# Yorkshire Wolds and the East Yorkshire Coast
## 40 favourite walks

The author and publisher have made every effort to ensure that the information in this publication is accurate, and accept no responsibility whatsoever for any loss, injury or inconvenience experienced by any person or persons whilst using this book.

published by
**pocket mountains ltd**
The Old Church, Annanside,
Moffat DG10 9HB

ISBN: 978-1-916739-13-0

Text copyright © J Fallis 2026
Photography copyright Derek Houghton © 2026

The right of J Fallis to be identified as the Author of this work has been asserted by him in accordance with the Copyright, Designs and Patents Act 1988

A catalogue record for this book is available from the British Library

Contains Ordnance Survey data © Crown copyright and database 2026

All rights reserved. No part of this publication may be reproduced, stored in a retrieval system, or transmitted in any form or by any means, electronic or mechanical, including photocopying and recording, unless expressly permitted by Pocket Mountains Ltd.

Printed by J Thomson Colour Printers, Glasgow

# Introduction

The term 'wold' derives from the Old English word *wald*, meaning 'forest' or 'high forest land'. When the forests were cleared by early farmers the name stuck and today these rolling uplands remain noticeably lacking in woodland, similar to the Lincolnshire Wolds across the Humber Estuary and the rounded grass-covered downlands of southern England. It could be said that the Yorkshire Downs would be a more apposite name, as *dun* in Old English means 'hill', but it is better to think of the Wolds as simply the northern version of the Downs.

The arc of low-lying hills that curves around from the Humber Estuary to the east Yorkshire coast to terminate where Flamborough Head meets the North Sea sits on the most northerly chalk bedrock in Britain. Like other English downlands, the bright white chalk is formed from the shell debris of a long-gone tropical sea. In marked contrast to the rolling hills of the Wolds, the former marshland of the Holderness Plain lies to the east and, to the west, the pastoral Vale of York. The Vale of Pickering, a former glacial lake, is to the north of the Wolds and is drained by the River Derwent, a natural boundary. For those who don't know the area well, these gentle northern wolds and the beaches and headlands of the east Yorkshire coast are somewhat overshadowed by the Yorkshire Dales and North York Moors. In contrast to the two long-established national parks, however, the hill summits here are not the main attraction; in fact, the cultivated plateaux are the least interesting feature. Instead it's the dry valleys, known as dales or slacks, formed in the periglacial period when streams and rivers were unable to sink into the frozen ground, which hold the key to this area and where the curious walker will find a much quieter tapestry of history, geology and natural beauty. The Great Wolds Valley is the widest and longest of these and features the delightfully named Gypsey Race, the most northerly chalk stream in Britain.

While farming remains as dominant as ever – the field tops above the valleys have been ploughed and planted with arable crops for hundreds of years – only plantations and shelter belts for farmhouses built following the enclosure of the vast sheep walks in the 18th and 19th centuries remain. In many ways, however, the Wolds have escaped the changes seen in other areas of Britain; a timelessness beautifully reflected in works by the celebrated Yorkshire-born artist David Hockney which have, in recent years, encouraged a greater appreciation of this unhurried yet ever-changing rural landscape.

For walkers, there are no great climbs or scrambles to be found here; instead, there is peace and quiet, big skies and solitude and plenty of uncrowded waymarked trails. Many of the walks in this book take in sections of long-distance walking routes such as the 127km-long Wolds Way which links Hessle and the Humber to Filey Brigg. Unsurprisingly, however, there is no long-distance coastal trail due to soft boulder clays which mean the rate of erosion on the Holderness coast is the fastest in Europe. Nevertheless, there are some stunning clifftop walks; the high chalk cliffs at Flamborough and Bempton, teeming with birdlife nesting on the tiniest of ledges, are simply unmissable.

### Early history

Alongside Orkney and Wessex, the Yorkshire Wolds is a key area for students of the Neolithic period when animals were domesticated and grains such as barley and wheat were cultivated. Good chalk soils along with stone suitable for crafting hand tools made this area very attractive to early settlers. Funerary monuments from this period are found across the Wolds but especially in the Great Wolds Valley. The massive 4000-year-old standing stone in Rudston churchyard is also a lasting legacy of ancient settlement.

The rich heritage of Bronze and Iron Age Wolds includes boundary earthworks, such as Dane's Dyke, which cuts across Flamborough Head, made by the first tribes. Barrows or burial mounds – of which there are more than 1400 – were often built for whole families or important leaders and filled with grave goods. Despite the advance of agriculture and repeated ploughing, many of these barrows remain upstanding. There is also evidence of early trading with near neighbours and with Rome in the late Iron Age period.

Yorkshire was first brought under Roman control in 43AD and the area has the most northerly concentration of villas in Roman Britain. The majority of these were built on, or close to, the western Wolds escarpment, with access to the provincial capital of Eboracum, which developed into the present-day York. By the mid 4th-century AD, however, signal stations were built along the Yorkshire coast at a time when the north of England was being invaded from across the North Sea.

In 410AD the Romans formally ended their occupation and Emperor Honorius withdrew the military defence of the province. Angles, Saxons and Jutes sporadically crossed the North Sea and in 627AD the Anglo-Saxon pagan King Edwin of Northumbria was baptised by Paulinus in York, an event that began the Christianisation of the region. In 866AD the 'Great Army' of the Angles captured York and founded more permanent settlements such as Wharram Percy – one of the most studied and celebrated settled sites in all of England – as well as the 'lost' villages of Cottam and Cowlam. Settlers from across the North Sea also left behind some unusual placenames, such as the wonderful Wetwang.

Poetry Bench near Huggate ▶

# Introduction

**Medieval Wolds**

Following the Norman Conquest of 1066, William the Conqueror set about the 'Harrying of the North' to bring rebellious nobles under control and in 1085 commissioned the Domesday Book to survey and record the value of the land and resources in his new kingdom.

Although no monasteries were founded in the Wolds, Cistercian monks established a grange at Wharram-le-Street within a day's journey of Meaux Abbey, near Beverley, and built farmsteads. Lay farmers as well as the monks were soon bringing produce to markets and fairs in the developing towns where there were churches, such as Driffield, Market Weighton and Pocklington, and the River Derwent which was used to transport wool to Hull. Driffield remains the home of the largest one-day agricultural show in Britain. During this time Beverley became one of the most important centres of trade and Christianity in England, and work began on the magnificent minster in 1220. Violent incursions by Scots led by King Robert the Bruce, following a failed invasion of Scotland by King Edward II in 1322, however, and the arrival of the catastrophic Black Death, via the Humber in 1349, had a devastating impact on the area and left many villages greatly reduced in size or deserted completely.

Despite the inaccessibility and remoteness of the Wolds, the region was

nevertheless involved in some of the most momentous political changes in England. The Pilgrimage of Grace in 1536 saw thousands from the Wolds march to York to protest against Henry VIII's attacks on the Catholic Church. Although there were no major battles fought here during the Civil War, Hull and York were strategically important and several skirmishes took place. Charles I's attempt to take control of the arsenal at Hull in April 1642 was one of the most significant events leading to the outbreak of war.

In the post-medieval period, the Wolds saw rapid periods of change. Common land was enclosed, people migrated to towns to earn wages in industry and ports such as Hull and Bridlington took advantage of foreign trade. Great estates expanded their landholdings, swallowing up villages, and vast deer parks were established for hunting.

By the middle of the 19th century most of the region was devoted to arable crops, while turnpike roads were established and canals were dug to connect market towns to navigable rivers; wheat, rye, malt, oats and barley were sent to London and coal, brick, lime and stone were imported the same way. It was not long before the railways changed everything, however; ports became better connected to markets, coastal holiday resorts developed and the importance of the market towns faded.

Into the 20th century, agriculture continued to dominate and despite machinery becoming more commonplace, horses remained important to the Wolds, primarily in farming, but also for sport;

◄ Beverley Minster

horse-racing and breeding dates back to the 17th century in the area. The region has also long been a popular tourist destination with holidaymakers flocking to the promenades and beaches of Bridlington, Filey and Withernsea from industrial towns during the summer.

**About this guide**
This guide contains 40 walks which are a mix of classics and less explored routes that have been selected to reveal more unexpected parts. Ranging in length from an hour's stroll to a day's walking, they are divided into four sections broadly based on the topography of the country. Most of the routes are circular and although some feature steeper ascents, in general they are on well-worn and waymarked paths which should require minimal time for route-finding. The descriptions concentrate on the salient points of navigation but may not cover every twist and turn. If in doubt the obvious path is usually the line to take. An illustrative map accompanies each route but for longer walks it is a good idea to refer to the relevant OS Explorer mapping, details of which are given at the start of each route.

The recommended time for each walk is an estimate based on an average walking speed of 4km per hour with allowances made for steeper or clifftop routes; not included in the times are refreshment breaks, wildlife spotting or stop-offs. Timings will also vary for the seasonal effects on paths. A few routes also pass along clifftops or follow rivers and stretches of coastline which can become inaccessible depending on rainfall or the tides. While signage and maintenance of the better-used and long-distance routes is generally good they can become overgrown in summer, often obscuring stiles and signage.

Many of the towns in the Wolds and on the coast make good bases for walkers and are fairly well-connected by bus services, although it is not always possible to access walks by public transport. If coming from the west by car there are three main roads radiating from York that offer access to the area. Parking can be a sensitive issue, however, especially in smaller villages, and there is often limited parking on more hard to access routes. Consideration should always be shown to the needs of local residents and the farming community. Don't block field access gates.

Dogs can be taken on most of these walks but need to be kept under control and on a lead through fields of livestock, sensitive wildlife habitats and where signs advise, especially at lambing time. It is also not unheard of for cows with calves to become protective of their young, and cattle just released from winter shelter should always be left well alone. If in doubt it is usually possible, and advisable, to look for a detour.

Flamborough Head ▶

**From the rocky peninsula** of Filey Brigg to the tidal island of Spurn Head at the mouth of the River Humber, the spectacular east Yorkshire coast is known for its soaring cliffs, impressive sea stacks, secluded coves and important wildlife habitats. Since Victorian times visitors have also made their way across the Holderness Plain to holiday in classic seaside towns like Filey, Bridlington and Withernsea and enjoy their busy harbour life, long promenades and glorious golden sand beaches.

The varied walks in this chapter include strolls around those charming resorts and explorations of some wonderful sites for spotting puffins, gannets and razorbills, as well as seals and porpoises at Flamborough Head, Bempton Cliffs, Filey Brigg, Dane's Dyke and the fascinating Spurn National Nature Reserve with its unique tidal and estuarine ecosystem. This coastline is also suffering erosion at the fastest rate of any in Europe and evidence of this can be seen most clearly on the beach walk at Barmston.

Remnants of early human activity, including prehistoric, Roman and medieval settlements, as well as wartime defences, can also be seen all along the 75km-long coast.

# East Yorkshire Coast

1. **Filey Brigg** — 10
   Leave the charming seaside town behind to walk along the top of a rocky wildlife-rich peninsula

2. **Filey** — 12
   Stroll through historic streets, promenades and gardens

3. **Hunmanby and Reighton Gaps** — 14
   March along the sands to inspect two natural weaknesses in Britain's wartime defences

4. **Bempton Cliffs** — 16
   Pack your binoculars for this spectacular clifftop trip to view the east Yorkshire coast's 'seabird city'

5. **Flamborough Head** — 18
   Take the high path around the famous headland with coves, caves, arches, beaches and seabird colonies all the way

6. **Dane's Dyke Nature Reserve** — 20
   Discover a stunning beach sheltered by gleaming white chalk cliffs at the end of an ancient defensive barrier

7. **Bridlington** — 22
   Enjoy the busy harbour life, long promenades and glorious sandy beaches of this resort town

8. **Barmston Sands** — 24
   Head out across farmland before strolling back on a long sandy beach

9. **Withernsea** — 26
   Explore the seafront of the welcoming coastal town before returning past an unusual inland lighthouse

10. **Spurn National Nature Reserve** — 28
    Marvel at the shifting seascape, huge skies and thriving wildlife found on this remarkable tidal island

EAST YORKSHIRE COAST

# Filey Brigg

**Distance** 3km **Time** 1 hour 15
**Terrain** pavement, paths, some steep steps and sandy beach **Map** OS Explorer 301
**Access** buses to Filey from Bridlington, Scarborough and York; trains from York, Hull, Beverley, Malton and Driffield

Filey Brigg is a long narrow peninsula with 20m-high fossil-rich limestone and chalk cliffs steeped in history and folklore. This short walk heads along the seafront of Filey before meandering up through a country park and along a clifftop path to Carr Naze and the rocky headland of the Brigg.

The walk starts from the roundabout near both the train and bus stations in Filey. (There are plenty of options for parking around town.) Head along Station Avenue through the centre of town, then go down Cargate Hill towards the sea. Look out for 'Bonzo the Recycling Seal', doing his bit to keep the beach clean, and turn left to pass a wonderfully detailed steel statue of a local fisherman by Ray Lonsdale called *High Tide in Short Wellies* – although locals know this imposing chap simply as Findlay.

Before you reach the lifeboat station by the slipway at Coble Landing, bear left to go briefly up Ravine Road and follow the steep steps off to the right. Climb the steps up the steep wooded slope and follow the path marked with the acorn symbol. Once up the steps continue along the top of the cliff until you approach a screen of trees. Go left here to pass a playpark and then turn right on the road by the café.

Continue past the toilet block, then

◀ Filey Brigg

return to the clifftop path and follow it through a gap in the fence to Carr Naze and the stone artwork marking the end of the Wolds Way, which begins 127km away at Hessle. This is also the end – or start – point of the 177km-long Cleveland Way which links Filey with Helmsley.

From here you can walk out along the Brigg to enjoy views back across Filey Bay and beyond. Five carved foundation stones of what was thought to be a 4th-century wooden watchtower built by Roman soldiers in order to spot marauding Saxons were discovered here in the 1870s. According to local legend the Brigg was either hammered into shape by the devil himself or was formed by the skeleton of a drowned dragon who once tormented the townsfolk. Always popular with birdwatchers, the cliffs and intertidal foreshore here attract oystercatchers, grebes and red-throated divers, as well as cormorants, shags and various gulls. If you are lucky you might spot grey seal, harbour porpoise or bottlenose dolphin.

To return to Filey, follow the Wolds Way back along the clifftop before dropping down to the beach at the slipway – if the tide is out – and walk back along the top of the beach to the start.

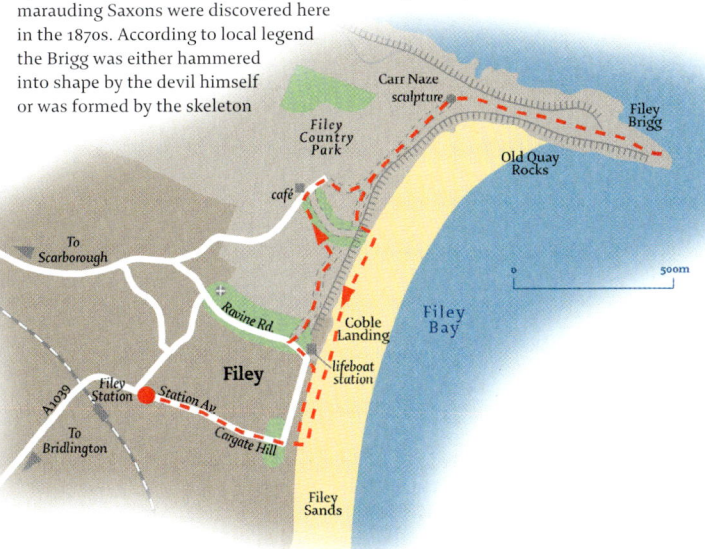

# Filey

**Distance** 2km **Time** 45 minutes
**Terrain** pavement and paths
**Map** OS Explorer 301 **Access** buses to Filey from Bridlington, Scarborough and York; trains from York, Hull, Beverley, Malton and Driffield

**Filey is the most southerly seaside resort in North Yorkshire and the charming town retains much of its fine Georgian, Victorian and Edwardian architecture. This short walk takes in the old town, the seafront and The Crescent, a gently curving terrace of tall white villas which recalls an era when Filey prided itself on being 'free from vulgarity' and routinely attracted holidaying politicians, writers, aristocrats and royals.**

Filey sits on a long sandy beach and the golden sands, sea air and saltwater first attracted tourists in the Georgian era. Following the arrival of the railway line in 1840, the town became a favourite with high society; Charles Dickens, Charlotte Brontë and Frederick Delius, as well as various members of Queen Victoria's family, were regular visitors. Fairground entrepreneur Billy Butlin opened his third camp, following others at Skegness and Clacton, to the south of the town in 1939; at its peak more than 175,000 happy campers visited for the season.

The walk starts from the roundabout near both the train and bus stations. (There is plenty of parking around the town.) Go along Station Road, then straight ahead onto Church Street to explore the oldest part of Filey. Just off to the right, down Queen Street is an award-winning local museum housed in a restored 17th-century fisherman's cottage.

Continue to cross Church Bridge. This once connected East and North Yorkshire; the whole town was moved into North Yorkshire in 1974. The wrought-iron

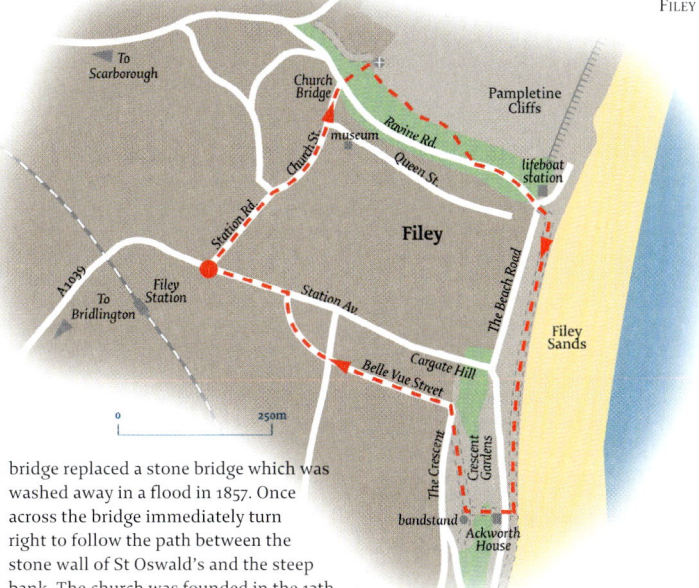

bridge replaced a stone bridge which was washed away in a flood in 1857. Once across the bridge immediately turn right to follow the path between the stone wall of St Oswald's and the steep bank. The church was founded in the 12th century and is said to have been used as a navigation point by local fishermen returning to the harbour and by sailors making their way from shipping yards on the Tyne, Esk and Wear to London. Dickens knew the graveyard well and wrote about the harsh living conditions of local families in the old town.

Follow the path down to Ravine Road (also known as the Church Ravine) and continue past the lifeboat station before turning right to walk along the seafront. Pass the tall steel statue of a fisherman and carry on until you see some steps across the road to the side of Ackworth House, a former seafront hotel dating from the 1860s.

Cross the road and go up the steps into the well-kept Crescent Gardens which are overlooked by one of the most architecturally impressive streets on the British coastline. Originally set out as a promenade around 1835 for the enjoyment of guests of the Royal Crescent Hotel and residents of The Crescent, the park and centrepiece bandstand remain as popular as ever with visitors.

Leave Crescent Gardens via the right-hand corner to join the road as it bends left into Belle Vue Street, which is lined with pubs, cafés and gift shops. Cross the road onto residential Belle Vue Crescent before turning left on Station Avenue to return to the start.

◀ Filey Sands

# Hunmanby and Reighton Gaps

**Distance** 10km **Time** 3 hours
**Terrain** pavements, paths, steep steps and sandy beach **Map** OS Explorer 301
**Access** no public transport to the start; buses from Bridlington to Reighton where you can join the route

Soon after the outbreak of World War Two the long sandy beach south of Filey was considered to be a potential landing site for a German invasion. This walk goes across farmland and through two quiet villages before returning along a seafront littered with old wartime pillboxes, anti-tank blocks and gun positions. Always be aware of the tide times to avoid being marooned between Reighton and Hunmanby Gaps.

Start this walk from the car park (charge) at Hunmanby Gap at the end of Sands Road off the roundabout on the A165 between Filey and Reighton. Head down the tarmac track towards the beach, then take the steep steps on the right up to the coastal path. Follow this as it trends inland and then runs along the edge of Reighton Sands Holiday Park.

Follow the signposts past the entrance to the park and continue on a tarmac track past a farm and along the side of a golf course. Arriving at a farm gate, turn right along the fence and make your way between the gorse bushes and through another gate, before emerging on the road by St Peter's Church in Reighton. Turn left on the road, on narrow pavements at

# HUNMANBY AND REIGHTON GAPS

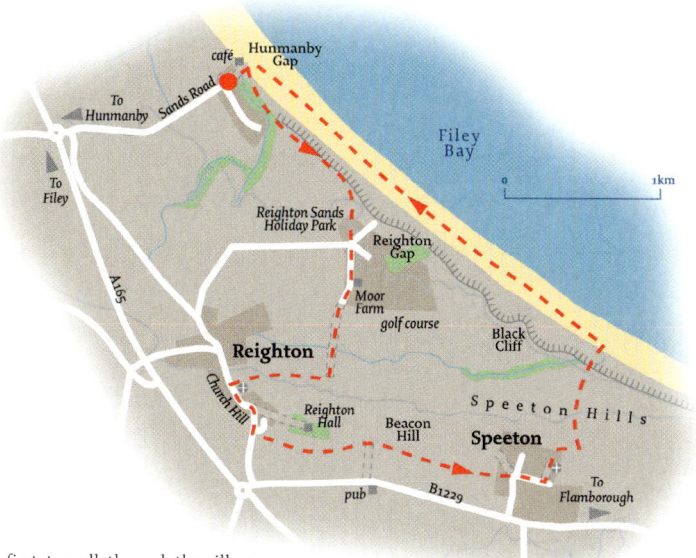

first, to walk through the village.

At the footpath sign just past Reighton Court, turn left to head along the edge of fields and around Beacon Hill, an MOD site, to eventually arrive in Speeton. Keep ahead through the village to reach the ornamental pond and the tiny Saxon church of St Leonard's, one of the smallest parish churches in Yorkshire. Inside there is a remarkable 1000-year-old font still in use.

To get to the beach, follow the signposts from here through gates and across fields. The final descent to the beach is steep and rugged so some care needs to be taken. To the north, at the end of the huge stretch of sand, is the popular seaside resort of Filey; to the south are the towering cliffs of Bempton, an RSPB sanctuary and home to some of the largest seabird colonies in the UK.

On the beach you will soon see various pieces of wartime debris embedded in the shifting sands as you make your way back to Hunmanby Gap. The only other break in the cliffs is at Reighton Gap below the holiday park; both defensive weak points were well covered by guns sited on the flanking clifftops during the war.

Once back at Hunmanby Gap it's a short climb back up to the car park via the seasonal Beach Café on the clifftop.

◀ Looking over Filey Bay towards Bempton Cliffs

# Bempton Cliffs

**Distance** 6.5km **Time** 2 hours
**Terrain** undulating grassy clifftop path
**Map** OS Explorer 301 **Access** buses and trains from Bridlington stop at Bempton, 2km from RSPB Bempton Cliffs visitor hub. There is a charge to enter the reserve for non-RSPB members

This out-and-back walk from the RSPB Bempton Cliffs visitor hub takes you along the top of some of the highest and most spectacular chalk cliffs in England. The cliffs are a magnet for birdwatchers, especially between March and August, when around half a million seabirds gather on the cliffs to raise their young. There are several well-fenced observation points for you to view the inhabitants of this fascinating 'seabird city'.

The walk starts and ends at the RSPB Bempton Cliffs visitor hub – where there is plenty of parking, toilets and a café – 2km north of the quiet village of Bempton. From the car park follow the signs towards the cliffs and bear left at the first junction of paths just beyond the RSPB building. Not far away are the eerie remains of an abandoned wartime RAF base which was the site for the testing of a secret high-speed radar system, codenamed 'Winkle', in the 1950s.

Once at the cliffs you can enjoy the protected viewing platforms to spot gannet, puffin, kittiwake, razorbill, fulmar, herring gull, shag and guillemot crowding the cliffs, especially during nesting season. There are more than 11,000 breeding pairs of migrating gannet which start arriving from West Africa each season from February onwards. These huge birds can travel over 300km on a fishing trip and the sight of thousands of them leaving together to look for cod, mackerel and herring is remarkable.

◀ Cliffs at Bempton

Another favourite of visitors is the puffin; they usually nest in burrows at other sites but here they make use of crevices and cracks in the soft chalk cliffs. Known as the 'clown of the seas' for their rainbow-coloured beaks and red eyes, they are part of the auk family and in winter turn more monochrome when they aren't trying so hard to attract a mate. At other times of the year corn buntings, skylarks and linnets breed in the grasslands and inland scrub, and kestrel, barn owls and short-eared owls can be seen hunting their prey.

Look out too for the geology of the cliffs; there are some alarming vertical incisions which are the result of the seawater working on weaknesses in the chalk. Horizontal weaknesses are the result of the weathering of the softer layers that are interleaved with layers of harder flint which weathers more slowly. The ledges that result are used by the seabirds for nesting.

Continue along the route as it undulates along the top of the cliffs; as the walk nears the turnaround you can enjoy views of Filey Bay to the north and inland to the high ground of the northern Wolds. Once at the trig point – a simple concrete pillar on the cliff edge – simply turn around and enjoy the views in the opposite direction back towards the RSPB hub and beyond to Flamborough.

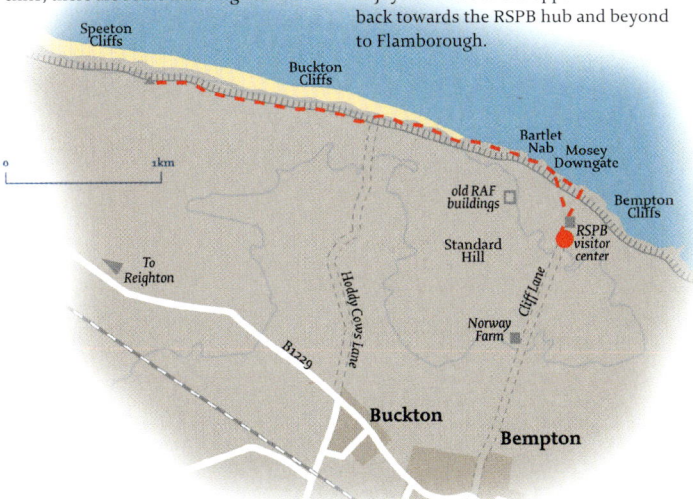

# Flamborough Head

**Distance** 12km **Time** 4 hours
**Terrain** pavement, tracks and clifftop paths with ascents and descents
**Map** OS Explorer 301 **Access** buses from Bridlington to Flamborough

With soaring chalk cliffs, secluded coves and caves, magnificent natural arches and one of the largest seabird colonies in Europe, this longer walk around the headland between Filey and Bridlington is the Yorkshire coast at its very best.

From the crossroads near St Oswald's Church in the village of Flamborough follow Church Street, then Tower Street, past the remains of Flamborough Castle. The medieval castle was seized by the crown in 1536 following the execution of Sir Robert Constable for his part in the Pilgrimage of Grace.

Continue through the village and along North Marine Road to a footpath just beyond the last of the houses. Follow this to the entrance of Thornwick Bay Holiday Village and bear right to pass the lifeboat. From here follow the tarmac track to the end, then turn right through a gate and continue on the path to the road which goes out to Thornwick Bay. Cross the road and take the path ahead, then go up some steps to join the coastal path, or continue down to visit Thornwick Bay first.

The next long uninterrupted stretch of the coastal path goes down the headland with superb views of the only chalk cliffs in the north of England all the way. Thousands of gannets, herring gulls, guillemots, razorbills, fulmars, kittiwakes and puffins return every year to nest here on the narrow ledges. Pods of harbour

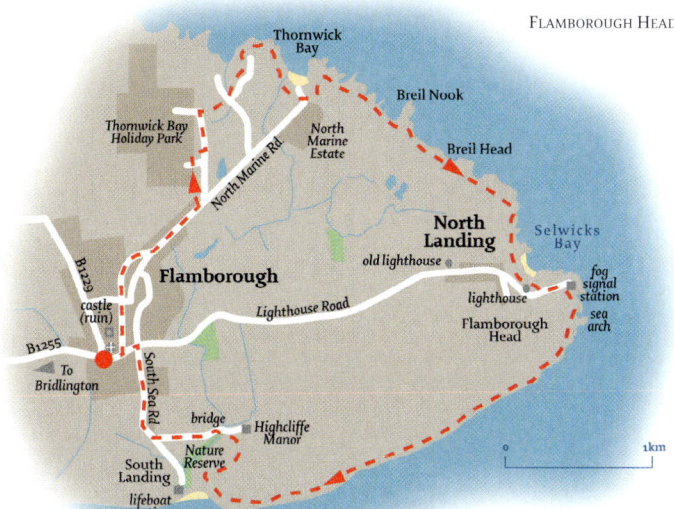

porpoises can also often be seen and occasionally dolphins and minke whales. Eventually North Landing hoves into view but first there is a slight drop into Holmes Gut before you reach the car park and café. Continue along the crenulated coastline, passing a golf course with a perilous 14th hole, to arrive at Flamborough Head's lighthouse, built in 1806 and still in service. An earlier lighthouse, built from chalk in 1669, still stands just inland.

From Flamborough Head carry on past the fog signal station above Selwicks Bay to meet 'the drinking dinosaur', a 30m-tall sea arch carved by the North Sea which – if you close your eyes a little bit – resembles a long-necked stegosaurus taking a gulp from the sea.

Continue along the coastal path towards South Landing with its RNLI lifeboat station and slipway. At a bench and viewing point, turn inland to explore a local nature reserve which features several interesting artworks inspired by local heritage. The reserve is also home to many species of wildflower and a rare colony of tree sparrows. Follow the footpath around into the woodland to cross the ravine via the ornate 'whale bridge' which features the names of whale species and local cobbles, the small flat-bottomed fishing boats designed for the shallow beaches of this stretch of coast.

Emerge from the reserve on the access road to Highcliffe Manor and turn left to continue to South Sea Road, from where you can turn left to go down to the lifeboat station at South Landing and the beach, or right to return to Flamborough.

◄ North Landing, Flamborough Head

# Dane's Dyke Nature Reserve

**Distance** 4km **Time** 1 hour 15
**Terrain** pavement, tracks and good paths
**Map** OS Explorer 301 **Access** buses from Bridlington to Flamborough

Dane's Dyke was a 4km-long defensive earthwork that stretched across the whole of the Flamborough promontory, constructed to protect Bronze Age settlements from seaborne invaders. This walk crosses farmland and goes along the top of the cliffs before visiting what was the southern end of the dyke, a wooded nature reserve and a white cobbled beach under fossil-rich cliffs.

Start the walk from the crossroads near St Oswald's Church in Flamborough and go down West Street. Keep ahead to the end of the street, then continue past Beacon Farm and the caravan site before continuing on a footpath along the edge of the field towards the sea. At the end, turn right to follow the high path enjoying great views along the cliffs towards Bridlington and beyond. Pass the concrete WWII pillbox sited precariously on the edge of the cliff before going down some steep steps to enter Dane's Dyke Nature Reserve.

At the bottom of the steps turn left for the beach and a paddle in the sea or right to continue along the path. The prehistoric dyke met the sea here and made use of the natural deep gully; for the rest of its length it was comprised of layers of chalk blocks, rubble and earth, covered with turf and topped with a wooden palisade fence, similar in

◀ The beach at Dane's Dyke

construction to Offa's Dyke on the Welsh border. It would have been a formidable barrier – up to 5m high in places. Despite the name, it was built in pre-Roman times, most likely during the Bronze Age, and not by Danish invaders.

You can explore more of the woodland or take the path which leads directly up to the main car park. This occupies the site of a long-gone country house, which explains the presence of the exotic trees, which were popular with wealthy Victorians, found in the reserve. The house's outbuildings are still standing and there is a seasonal kiosk café and public toilets.

To return to Flamborough, follow the road signposted as the way out before crossing a footbridge to a path which runs alongside the road. This soon branches right to cross fields, with Flamborough's church tower and lighthouses visible in the distance. Turn right on Water Lane to return to West Street and the start.

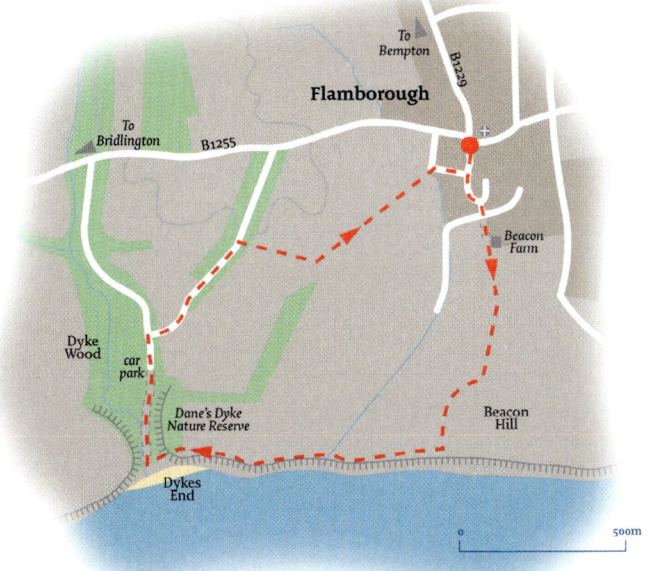

# Bridlington

**Distance** 4km **Time** 1 hour 15
**Terrain** pavement and promenade
**Map** OS Explorer OL17 **Access** buses and trains from Filey, Driffield, York and Hull to Bridlington

Bridlington is a lively seaside town which developed from a small fishing port to become one of the most popular resorts on the Yorkshire coast following the discovery of a chalybeate spring in the 19th century. This walk takes in some of the town's Edwardian terraces, the long promenade and the bustling harbour.

Start from Station Square by the railway station and walk towards Hilderthorpe Road, stepping over the flowing Gypsy Race as you go. Cross the road and head down terraced Olinda Road, then go right, first left, left again and then right down Neptune Street to meet South Marine Drive. Across the road, the Bridlington Spa is an historic venue with an art deco ballroom and an ornate Edwardian theatre that has seen its fair share of stars. The Who, David Bowie, The Rolling Stones and The Clash, among many others, have packed out the famous Spa; Manchester rockers Oasis played their last indoor concert here in 2009.

Go down South Marine Drive, then take the ramp onto the promenade. Turn left to pass the RNLI lifeboat station and the rear of the theatre and head towards the

harbour. Carry on along the seafront, then go up the ramp above the harbour and look out for *The Anchorman*, a sculpture on top of the Harbour Commissioners building by Ronald Falck which celebrates the local harbour workers. Known as the 'Lobster Capital of Europe', Bridlington's harbour has a long history of shellfish fishing and around 300 tonnes of lobster are landed here every year.

Bear right to go through the car park and head along the walkway beside the water. At the red sea mine turn right to detour along the sea wall, passing the *Gansey Girl*, a bronze statue by artist Steve Carvill. The young woman is knitting a traditional heavy woollen fisherman's jersey originally made on the Channel island of Guernsey, hence the name 'gansey'. The gansey was adopted by mainland coastal areas with villages and families developing their own unique and distinctive patterns. Names of local fishing families are engraved on the fish which swim around beneath the statue.

Back on the promenade, pass the amusements and the leisure centre and a shelter decorated with ornate black wrought iron, then leave the seafront by the steps to go up Albion Terrace. At the end, turn left, then right onto Tennyson Avenue and continue down Wellington Road to the war memorial. Bear right onto Quay Road and go down Station Approach just before the level crossing to return to the railway station.

◀ Bridlington's *Gansey Girl*

# Barmston Sands

**Distance** 5.5km **Time** 1 hour 45
**Terrain** tracks, paths and sandy beach
**Map** OS Explorer 292 **Access** buses from
Bridlington to Barmston

Just south of Bridlington, the village of Barmston is the start and finish point for this walk of two halves which returns along the golden sands of Barmston beach. Due to the soft clay in the low cliffs of this stretch of the Holderness coast there is a great deal of ongoing erosion and it is best to return on a low tide when the beach is at its widest.

From the pond in the middle of Barmston, head along the road towards the coast and turn left onto Hamilton Hill Road. Keep straight on as the tarmac becomes a farm track and leaves the houses behind. At the junction before the farm, bear right and meander around the high ground of Hamilton Hill and past a WWII pillbox, one of around 28,000 built in Britain during the course of the war in anticipation of a German invasion. Continue along the edge of fields to eventually meet the Earl's Dike, an ancient land drain on the edge of the parish boundary. Turn right and follow this to the beach.

There is often no obvious path onto the beach so take care making your way down. From April to September the low cliffs here are home to pairs of nesting sand martins which burrow into the soft rock. On the way back along the coast

look out too for the anti-tank defences that were placed across the beach to deter and channel tanks and other vehicles. During a storm in 1967 around 6m of coastline was lost here over two days and in 1978 some of the blocks were (unsuccessfully) re-purposed to try and slow down the rate of erosion and protect properties at risk of falling into the sea from the headland at Barmston.

Despite the construction of groynes and breakwaters, little can be done to stop the natural processes of the tides, winds and waves, and going further back it is estimated that since Roman times at least 30 settlements have been lost to the sea along the Yorkshire coast. Due to rising sea levels and the effects of climate change, however, there is little doubt that the rate of erosion is increasing, and the area is now recognised as having the fastest eroding coastline in Europe.

Just before reaching the holiday park there is an obvious way off the beach. Follow the signposts and make your way to Sands Lane which leads back to Barmston and the start.

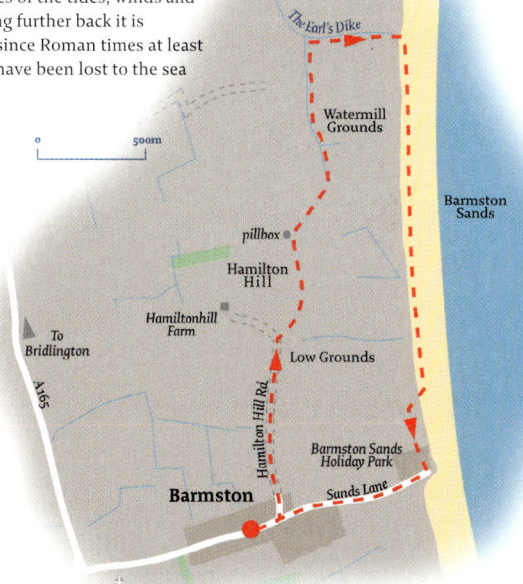

# Withernsea

**Distance** 4km **Time** 1 hour 15
**Terrain** pavement and promenade
**Map** OS Explorer 292 **Access** buses from Hull and Hornsea to Withernsea

As well as golden sands and all the usual seaside attractions, the traditional Yorkshire coastal town of Withernsea has a pair of more interesting historical landmarks. This easy stroll around the town starts and finishes on Withernsea's long promenade.

Start this walk from the wonderful twin castellated Pier Towers at the seaward end of Pier Road. As the names suggests, the town did once have a grand Victorian pier but it suffered through its short life from successive storms and ship collisions and was finally demolished in 1903; only the yellow-brick twin towers from the pier entrance remain.

Walk south along the promenade to pass the RNLI lifeboat station, looking out for points on the Fish Trail and the Fossil Furlongs. The Fish Trail starts at the crab sculpture on the promenade and consists of 12 points around town; the Fossil Furlongs are engravings of Jurassic period fossils mounted on reclaimed groynes every 200m (or one furlong) along the town's promenade.

Beyond the lifeboat station and the fishing lake, head inland along the residential Seacroft Road to Queen Street and turn right. Withernsea's octagonal lighthouse soon bobs in and out of view as you walk through town. Turn left onto

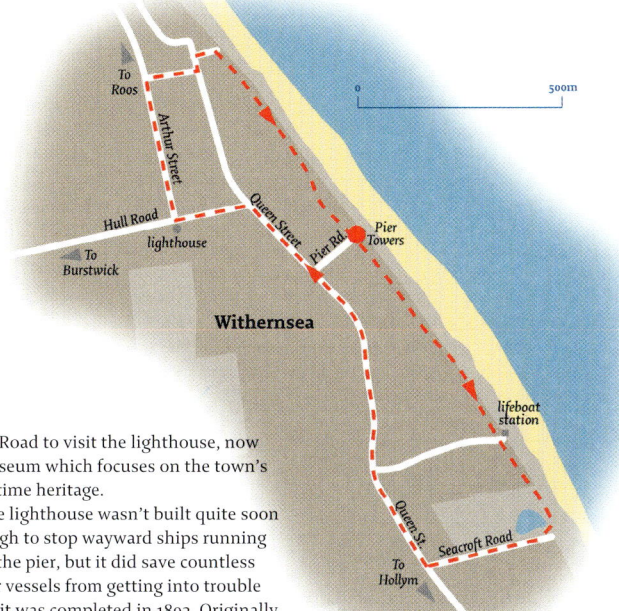

Hull Road to visit the lighthouse, now a museum which focuses on the town's maritime heritage.

The lighthouse wasn't built quite soon enough to stop wayward ships running into the pier, but it did save countless other vessels from getting into trouble after it was completed in 1892. Originally sited a good distance from the sea, the land between was soon built over and it was left strangely stranded amongst houses. After 80 years of invaluable service the light was finally switched off in 1976.

From the lighthouse, continue along Arthur Street and turn right onto Hubert Street, then turn left and right to reach the northern promenade. The long and wide promenades of Withernsea followed the arrival of the single-track railway line in 1854 which connected the town to Hull Victoria Dock station. This brought thousands of factory workers and their families over the Holderness Plain to enjoy an affordable holiday by the sea.

From here return to Pier Towers, looking out for an information board that illustrates the history of erosion on this coast. The original villagers of Withernsea relocated further inland as their first settlement and church had to be abandoned in 1444. The residents of the nearby settlement of Owthorne joined them in 1816 when their church was also washed away.

◀ Withernsea's old Pier Towers

# Spurn National Nature Reserve

**Distance** 14km **Time** 4 hours 30 **Terrain** concrete track, paths and sandy beach **Map** OS Explorer 292 **Access** no public transport to the start other than a seasonal bus (Spurn Explorer) from Hull or Patrington to Kilnsea (weekends and bank holidays only)

The wild, exposed and ever-changing tidal island at the end of the Holderness coast which curves between the North Sea and the Humber Estuary is popular with adventurous walkers and birdwatchers. The mix of habitats at Spurn attract a wide range of bird species, including rare visitors, and there is an historic lighthouse as well as reminders of the area's military history to explore. The walk can only be done at low tide so always check tide times before setting off. In order to protect the sensitive habitat and wildlife, no dogs are allowed.

Start from the Yorkshire Wildlife Trust's Discovery Centre, where there is parking (charge), excellent information about the National Nature Reserve and a café. Please do not park on the access road. From the centre, go to the end of the road, then continue towards the sand.

In December 2013 Spurn became an island when a huge tidal surge washed through the narrowest part of the peninsula. The soft sand and strong currents of water on the 'washover' section mean it can be very dangerous to cross at high tide. **No attempt to cross should be made until any water present has completely receded.**

After crossing the narrowest section and passing the high tide shelter, follow the concrete track towards the lighthouse. The haphazard steel tracks which criss-cross the route are the remains of a light railway line that ran to Spurn Head

## SPURN NATIONAL NATURE RESERVE

between 1915 and 1952. The track soon passes by a protected area of seagrass being restored as part of a project to improve the biodiversity of the Humber Estuary. The peninsula is designated as a Site of Special Scientific Interest and there are a series of hides to visit on the way to the lighthouse. The estuary is of international importance for the huge numbers of wildfowl and wading birds which visit at various times of year; the saltmarsh, dunes, grassland, saline lagoons, mudflats and scrubland offer a wide variety of welcoming habitats.

Eventually you arrive at the distinctive black and white Spurn lighthouse. Built in 1895 and decommissioned after 90 years of service, it has been restored and is open to the public. The nearby VTS Tower controls traffic on the Humber and houses built for the only full-time RNLI lifeboat crew in the British Isles are up ahead by the pier; in 2023 the lifeboat station was relocated to Grimsby. Further along, an old First World War gun emplacement overlooking the Humber can be explored.

Continue to the end of Spurn Point, marked with a global signpost, to see large cargo ships and passenger ferries passing by in the shipping lanes. Adult grey seals can often be seen here bobbing around in the water, and at certain times of the year their young appear on the beaches. They are protected wild animals, so always keep your distance.

After looping back around the headland, return the same way along the track. Once over the narrow stretch of sand, bear right to visit the seawatch hide where wildlife-watchers with telescopes look out over the water for passing dolphins and whales, as well as migrating birds, before walking back up the road to the Discovery Centre and the start.

◂ Spurn Head

Sir Tatton Sykes depicted on horseback on his monument ▶

**The northern part** of the Wolds feature the typical scenery of undulating farmland bisected by steep-sided dry valleys littered with prehistoric tumuli, mysterious earthworks and abandoned villages. The Great Wolds Valley is also home to the Gypsey Race, a seasonal chalk stream which features in local folklore due to its seemingly random appearance and disappearance at points along the valley.

The walks here and on the Holderness Plain feature plenty of big country houses, handsome churches and isolated villages. The rich history of the Vikings in Yorkshire outside of York is reflected in the names of places like Wetwang and Thwing and the impact of the devastating Black Death which swept through the area in the 14th century can be seen in the faint traces of lost villages such as Cottam and Cowlam. Changes in agricultural land use also had a big impact on the local population and the towering monument to Tatton Sykes, a local Victorian landowner who built many churches and rural schools to soften the impact of this social upheaval, is a local landmark.

The last walk shadows Hornsea Mere, the largest freshwater lake in Yorkshire, which sits just inland from the East Riding coast.

# Holderness and the Northern Wolds

**1 Fordon** 32
Tour a typical north Wolds landscape littered with Neolithic round barrows

**2 Thwing and Octon** 34
Travel through history on this easy circuit of farmland and tranquil villages

**3 West Lutton and Thirkleby Rattle** 36
Go with the flow on this rolling circuit which starts by walking along a celebrated winterbourne stream

**4 Cottam and Cowlam** 38
Pass through a pair of long-deserted settlements and steep-sided valleys formed in the last ice age

**5 Rudston** 40
Make your way from a huge monolith to follow bridleways and the line of an old Roman road through farmland

**6 Wetwang and the Sykes Monument** 42
Follow field paths and old drove roads to visit an imposing tribute to a benevolent Victorian landowner

**7 Bainton** 44
Start this circuit from an impressive church in a peaceful village and return along a stretch of the Minster Way

**8 Driffield, Wansford and Nafferton** 46
Stroll along the old canal looking out for kingfishers and heron to reach two villages, each with an interesting history

**9 Foston on the Wolds** 48
Open the door to a fine waterside walk alongside a rare chalk stream

**10 Hornsea Mere** 50
Look over the freshwater lake and visit an isolated Georgian church

# Fordon

**Distance** 6km **Time** 2 hours
**Terrain** country roads, tracks and paths
**Map** OS Explorer 301 **Access** no public transport to the start

This walk through typical northern Wolds countryside begins in the tranquil hamlet of Fordon, home to one of the smallest active churches in Britain. Part of the route follows the Wolds Way and passes by the site of a Neolithic round barrow, one of a remarkable number in this area.

Start the walk from the crossroads in Fordon (there is limited parking opposite the church or by the crossroads). The charmingly compact Church of St James dates from Norman times and is said to have been a hide-out for smugglers in the 18th and early 19th centuries who were landing contraband tea, tobacco, gin, brandy and silk on the deserted east coast and selling it to local communities inland. The church is not open to the public.

From the crossroads, head towards Ganton until you reach a red phonebox and postbox. Go through the yard of Low Fordon Farm and follow the footpath as it meanders along the bottom of North Dale. After arriving at an incongruous set of rugby posts continue past the access track for North Fordon Farm and carry on to enter Lang Dale.

Continue along the bottom of the dale to reach a signpost for the Wolds Way and head right up the steepening slope. After the short stiff climb to the road look out for a clump of trees on the far side of the field opposite.

◀ Church of St James, Fordon

This is Sharpe Howe, the overgrown site of a Neolithic round barrow, one of the important Folkton Barrow Group of funerary sites discovered in 1889 by Willian Greenwell, a canon of Durham Cathedral. One of these sites is where the 'Folkton Drums' were discovered in the grave of a young boy thought to have been from an important family. Now in the British Museum, the three enigmatic intricately carved chalk cylinders were possibly measuring devices that were used in the construction of Neolithic monuments such as Stonehenge around 5000 years ago.

Turn right to follow the road and enjoy the wonderful views as they open out in all directions; on a clear day Bempton Cliffs and the sea are visible. Continue along this quiet road with wide verges. Once beyond the entrance to Danebury Manor the road descends through a narrow wooded valley that is rich in seasonal wildflowers. The road eventually returns to the start at Fordon.

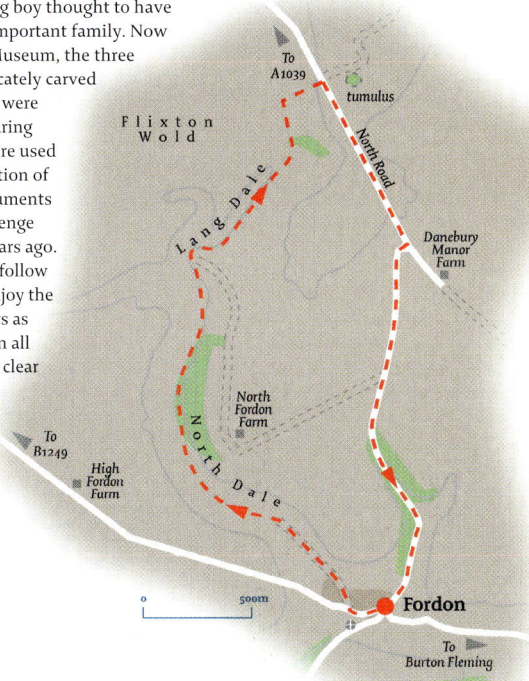

# Thwing and Octon

**Distance** 5.5km **Time** 1 hour 40
**Terrain** country roads, tracks and paths
**Map** OS Explorer 295 **Access** bus from Bridlington to Thwing

Reflecting the rich Viking history of this part of East Yorkshire, the wonderfully named village of Thwing (meaning 'strip of high land' in Old Scandinavian) is the starting point for this short time-travelling route.

From the crossroads in Thwing, walk down Butts Lane and bear right onto wide-verged Octon Road. Enjoy the views across the valley as you make your way along the quiet road before turning right at the end for Octon Grange.

You will soon pass a rare surviving example of a cruck house at Old Octon Farm. Simply constructed using pairs of long matching timbers connected at the top with a 'saddle', and in the middle with a 'collar', to form an A-shape, these structures were common in Yorkshire from the early Middle Ages. The timbers used in this building have been dated to around 1670.

Follow the signpost down the side of the more modern farmhouse and walk along the field edge path back to the road into Thwing. Cross the road to continue along the access track of Lampugh House. The former rectory is named after Thomas Lampugh, an Octon-born churchman who was fortuitously made Archbishop of York for his loyalty to King James II, the last Catholic monarch of England, Scotland and Ireland, just before he was deposed in the Glorious Revolution of 1688.

From the tarmac area walk across the field to the wooden gate and cross the next field, aiming for All Saints Church. Dating from the 12th century, the church retains several Norman features including

◀ All Saints Church, Thwing

a beautifully carved tub font and a tympanum above the south doorway depicting the Paschal lamb (representing Jesus Christ, or *Agnus Dei*, the Lamb of God) beneath a zigzag arch. The church's turret clock is also interesting; it has an unusual escarpment and was made in 1840 by James Harrison of Hull, the great-grandson of John Harrison, inventor of the marine chronometer who was celebrated in the first bestselling book about horology, *Longitude* by Dava Sobel.

Go left around Church Lane and keep left as the road bends right. Continue down the dead-end road past Little Farm, through the yard of Highfield Farm and across the field. Turn right at the road, then left to Thwing Mere. This was once the village's water supply and is now a peaceful wildlife haven. From the mere, make your way along Main Street to the start.

On the way look out for the former pub called The Falling Stone. This was named after the Wold Cottage Meteorite which fell to earth across the valley in 1795. Part of the 25kg meteorite – the largest observed to fall in Britain and the second largest in Europe – can be seen in the British Museum.

# West Lutton and Thirkleby Rattle

**Distance** 6km **Time** 2 hours
**Terrain** country roads, tracks and paths
**Map** OS Explorer 301 **Access** no public transport to the start

The pretty village of West Lutton is found in the Great Wold Valley, aka The Valley of Kings, the largest and broadest of the Yorkshire Wolds. This walk around rolling farmland is rich in the history and folklore of the area and begins by following the famous seasonal stream known as the Gypsey Race which flows through the valley from Wharram-le-Street to the North Sea at Bridlington.

Start the walk from St Mary's Church and walk alongside the Gypsey Race to the sharp bend in the road and continue to leave the village by Malton Lane.

The Gypsey Race gets its name from the fact that the winterbourne stream occasionally floods when the often-underground and therefore invisible stream quickly rises above the water table; 'gypsey' in local dialect means unexpected or sudden. Also known as the 'Waters of Woe', the stream has the ominous habit of flooding just before catastrophic events. It is said to have burst its banks just before the arrival of the Black Death, the outbreak of the English Civil War, the bad harvest of 1861 and before both World Wars and the hard winters of 1947 and 1962. There are similar streams in chalky areas of Kent and Hampshire.

At the junction with Low Road carry on following the sign for Settrington and continue along the quiet road as it gently ascends towards the wood visible ahead. At the turning for Linton Wold Farm look

left for a path into the woods and follow it along the field edge down to the road. This part of the walk crosses Thirkleby Rattle, the unusual name perhaps referring to the sound made by the fast-flowing Gypsey Race. Thirkleby was a medieval settlement which probably disappeared when the bubonic plague hit Yorkshire in the 14th century.

Leave the field at Low Road near Thirkleby Manor, a grade II listed Victorian house built on the site of a 10th-century dwelling said to have belonged to a granddaughter of Lady Godiva, who was exiled on the charge of treason in 1055 by Edward the Confessor. Cross the road and follow an often overgrown path alongside the Gypsey Race back to West Lutton.

If you have time it is worth visiting the well-appointed St Mary's which was designed in the elaborate Victorian Gothic Revival style by George Edmund Street, the architect also responsible for the Royal Courts of Justice on the Strand in London. No expense was spared by Sir Tatton Sykes, the wealthy local landowner who paid for it all.

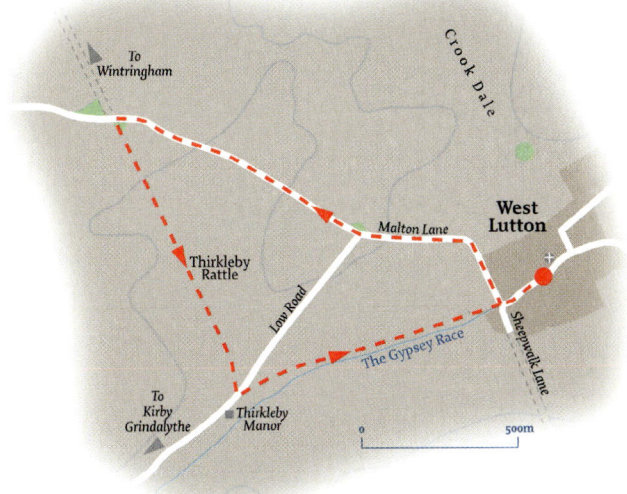

◀ West Lutton farmland

HOLDERNESS AND THE NORTHERN WOLDS

# Cottam and Cowlam

**Distance** 9km **Time** 3 hours
**Terrain** country roads, tracks and paths
**Map** OS Explorer 300 **Access** no public transport to the start

**This walk links two long-deserted villages via a maze of extraordinary uniformly V-shaped valleys created when the glaciers of the most recent ice age melted.**

The route starts at Church Farm near Cowlam Manor, east of Sledmere off the B1253 (limited parking north of the manor). Follow the footpath sign through the farmyard, passing the hard-to-miss St Mary's Church surrounded by well-preserved brick farm buildings. The old medieval village of Cowlam was located around here and was much reduced when the bubonic plague, also known as the Black Death or the Great Mortality, swept through in 1349. By 1690 only the parson and two shepherds were left.

The footpath leads into Cowlam Well Dale; directions are easy to follow with plenty of signs also telling you where not to go. Once in the bottom of the dale simply continue ahead enjoying the solitude and glimpses of wildlife. This steep-sided valley was formed because a river once flowed over the top of the frozen landscape; when everything melted at the end of the last ice age, the porous chalk under the river let the water go underground, leaving the valley 'dry'. Only in very wet weather do the rivers sometimes flow again.

The path eventually reaches a T-junction of path and dale. Turn left to follow the

# COTTAM AND COWLAM

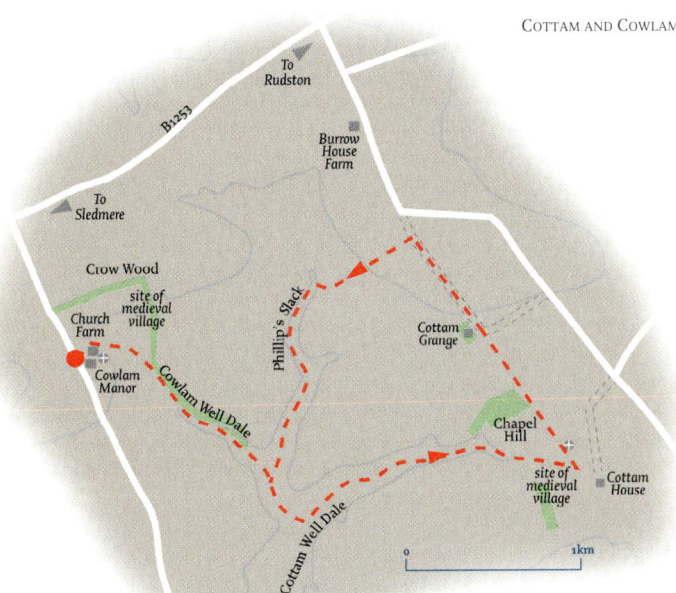

path into Cottam Well Dale and continue until it begins to gently ascend to the deserted church that becomes visible on the skyline.

This is the ruin of Holy Trinity Church, all that is left of the village of Cottam. In 1743 only one family was recorded as living here; it is thought everyone else left as more profitable sheep rearing replaced arable farming and the congregation became scattered around the dales. The old cultivation terraces which once supported the village can still be seen nearby.

From the ruins, turn left and walk to a gate and follow the footpath along the edge of a field towards a house. Once near Cottam Grange follow the signs to exit the farmyard onto a vehicle track.

Walk along the track to a footpath sign pointing left and follow this onto a chalk track. When the track turns sharply left, continue straight ahead and go through a gate to descend steeply to the bottom of this new dale, the marvellously named Phillip's Slack. Slack is another term for a V-shaped valley.

At the bottom go through a further gate, then turn left to follow the path along the bottom of the dale. This path meanders through the Slack until it reaches a fence and farm gate at a T-junction of dales. Go through the gate and turn right to retrace your steps to the start.

◂ Ruin of Holy Trinity Church, Cowlam

# Rudston

**Distance** 7km **Time** 2 hours 15
**Terrain** country roads, tracks and paths
**Map** OS Explorer 295 **Access** limited buses
to Rudston from Driffield and Bridlington

This walk explores the northern Wolds landscape around the peaceful village of Rudston, home to the tallest prehistoric standing stone in Britain. It also visits Woldgate, the old Roman road to Bridlington, which features in a number of paintings by David Hockney.

Start from All Saints Church in Rudston with the unmissable 7.5m-high 26-tonne Rudston Monolith in its grounds. There is some room to park opposite the church. Thought to extend just as far under the ground, legend has it that the devil was so angry that a church had been built here that he threw the stone and was slightly off with his aim. The name Rudston derives from the Old English word *rood-stane* or cross stone.

Go down School Lane, past the gate to the church and, just before Middle Street, bear left to follow the Gypsey Race to the village hall. Keep straight on with the stream through the trees to the road and turn right along East Gate over the bridge. On Long Street turn left, then left again onto South Side Lane which soon becomes a track. Keep on along the sunken lane, then turn right to follow the bridleway and keep the woods on the left as the views open out and height is gained.

The bridleway eventually meets the old Roman road called Woldgate, which linked Bridlington and York. David Hockney made the road famous with his celebrated *The Arrival of Spring* collection

◂ Rudston's church and monolith

based on sketches made with his iPad.

Head left along the road until you see a metal gate and signpost, then turn left to leave Woldgate on another bridleway. Look left and on the horizon, between the mobile mast and water tank, is a prehistoric burial mound where the bones of a young woman and infant were found, one of the many Neolithic and Bronze Age sites in the area. Continue along the way as it bends left, looking out for distant Thorpe Hall, a listed building dating from the 1740s.

Continue to follow signs into trees, then follow the edge of the wood between two fences and bear left before turning right at the next woodland to follow partially sunken land downhill.

After rejoining the outbound leg back, follow the second track right through the farm and between houses. Walk to the road junction, then turn right to cross the bridge and left to follow the stream back to Middle Street. Turn right along School Lane to return to All Saints Church and Rudston's mighty monolith.

# Wetwang and the Sykes Monument

**Distance** 9.5km **Time** 3 hours
**Terrain** country roads, tracks and paths
**Map** OS Explorer 294 **Access** limited buses to Wetwang from Driffield

The marvellously named village of Wetwang, west of Driffield on the A166 road, is the start point for this farmland walk to visit a soaring monument to a local Victorian landowner.

Start the walk from the village pond on the corner of Main Street and Station Hill in Wetwang. Go along Station Hill, looking out for a footpath and follow this through the houses, then go across the play area to a gap in the far hedge. Turn left, then right at the next hedge, and finally left at a path junction to arrive at a tarmac track. Turn right along the track to pass Station Farm, formerly a station on the old railway line linking Malton and Driffield.

Continue along the track to the entrance of Grange Farm and follow the signage to skirt around it. Carry on in the same direction as before across the foot of two fields to reach a farm track. Turn left along this until it bends right, then go through the woodland and keep straight on uphill to reach the deeply-rutted green lane which leads to the monument.

Erected in 1865, the landmark Sykes Monument is a towering neo-Gothic tribute to Sir Tatton Sykes, 4th Baronet of Sledmere (1772–1863). The elaborate 37m-high tower was designed by John Gibbs, who specialised in such memorials – he also designed Banbury Cross in Oxfordshire – and has a very narrow internal staircase. The tower originally had a full-time caretaker

# WETWANG AND THE SYKES MONUMENT

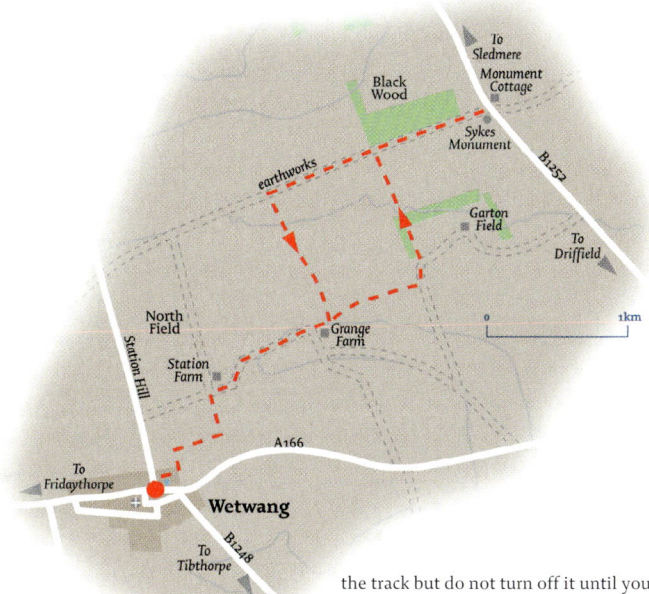

who took visitors to the viewing room at the top; his cottage is across the road but the staircase is no longer accessible.

Although Sir Tatton funded the building of several schools and rural churches in the Wolds, and his tenants paid for the monument after his death, he was reputedly an extremely puritanical and often cruel man who wore old-fashioned dress all his life. Among the detailed stone carvings on the monument is a sculptured relief of the baronet on horseback beneath a tree.

To return to Wetwang, go back along the track but do not turn off it until you reach a metal farm gate and a bridleway sign. From here, cross the field to the edge of Grange Farm again and follow the outbound route back to the start.

Wetwang hit the headlines in April 2001 when archaeologists uncovered the remains of the oldest Iron Age chariot ever found during a routine survey of a building plot here. The discovery of several other significant burial sites in the area confirmed the theory that this part of Yorkshire was settled around 400BC by the French-Celtic Parisi tribe, who originated in the Champagne region of northeast France and gave Paris its name.

# Bainton

**Distance** 6km **Time** 2 hours
**Terrain** country roads and tracks
**Map** OS Explorer 294 **Access** buses to Bainton from Driffield

Bainton is a small village on the edge of the Wolds with an impressive Gothic church known locally as the 'Cathedral of the Wolds'. This signposted circuit crosses flat farmland and an old country estate before returning over higher ground with good views across the valley.

Start the walk from the faded milestone in the wall of St Andrew's Church in Bainton. Parking can be found just north of the village in a large lay-by on the A614; buses from Driffield stop at the southern end of the village.

Parts of the church date from the 13th century, but it was almost completely rebuilt after a Scottish army swept through and ransacked it during the Great Raid of 1332. This was Robert the Bruce's bloodiest incursion into the north of England and followed Edward II's failed invasion of Scotland when his soldiers destroyed Holyrood Abbey in Edinburgh and the great border abbeys at Melrose and Dryburgh on their retreat. The church also contains the tomb of Edmund de Mauley, a local noble who never made it back from the Battle of Bannockburn in 1314. With such a history, it's surprising that the church is dedicated to Scotland's patron saint.

Walk along Applegarth Lane to leave the village on a single-track road (Neswick Lane) which meanders through farmland

◀ St Andrew's Church, Bainton

and parkland. The grand manor house of Neswick Hall no longer exists; what remains is its walled kitchen garden with restored glasshouses and vinery, the old home farm and stables, now residential housing, and many of the trees planted as part of a typical mid-18th century planned parkland. Some earthworks from a much earlier medieval settlement and old field furrows can also be seen.

Continue past Neswick Farm, then turn right on the road to soon cross the bridge over the long-gone Selby to Driffield railway line. Look out for the signpost further along the road and turn right to follow the edge of the field. The views start to widen either side of the path as you carry on to join a track through a strip of trees. This is part of the Minster Way, an 80km-long walking route between the Minster Churches of York and Beverley.

The track soon joins a road which leads to the A614 through Bainton. Follow the busy road to the wooden bus shelter and continue along quieter Church Street to return to St Andrew's Church.

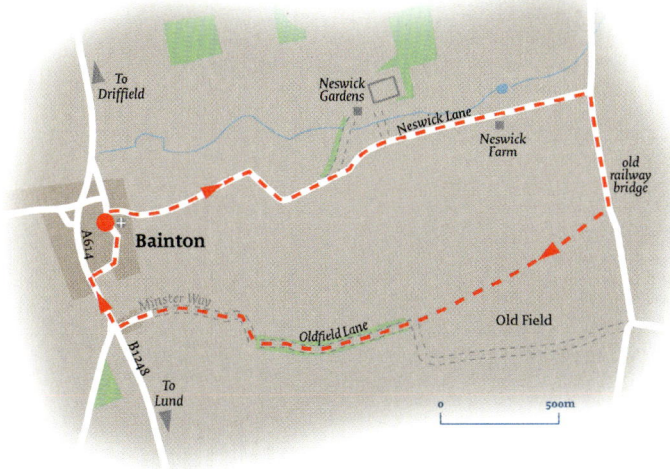

# Driffield, Wansford and Nafferton

**Distance** 11km **Time** 3 hours 20
**Terrain** country roads, canalside paths and tracks **Map** OS Explorer 295
**Access** buses to Driffield from Hull and Beverley; trains from Hull and Bridlington

With easy access to the Yorkshire Wolds, the market town of Driffield is known as the 'Capital of the Wolds' and is linked with Beverley and the Humber by the Driffield Navigation canal and the River Hull. This route explores the countryside and villages east of the town and follows the old canal, which closed to commercial traffic in 1951, for the first section.

Start from the junction of Riverhead, the town's former commercial centre, and Riverside, just beside the town's railway station. Walk south on Riverside along the canal past the converted warehouses, old grain mills and cranes to reach a kissing gate after passing the old town lock. Continue between the meandering clear headwaters of the River Hull and the canal on a winding path to reach the bridge, locks and weir at Whinhill Lock.

Cross over the canal to follow a path maintained by the Driffield Navigation Trust that runs along between the road and the canal, looking out for kingfishers and heron, to eventually reach the village of Wansford. In the 18th century a carpet weaving factory was set up here and orphaned children from London were brought to work the looms.

At the roundabout turn left to follow Nafferton Road into the village and continue past St Mary's Church, then take the next right onto Carr Lane. Follow this over a bridge and immediately turn left to follow the drainage ditch, Nafferton Beck. Eventually the path meets a road where you turn left to cross the water, then right to join a footpath and cross the railway line with care. Keep on the path along the edge of the fields with All Saints Church visible in the distance.

The path ends at a gate onto Priestgate; follow this past Nafferton Mere, the old mill pond of Nafferton Mill and now a pretty spot to enjoy wildlife in the middle of the village. Turn left at the church onto Westgate and follow this road away from the village until it turns sharply right. Join a footpath directly ahead which goes around a builder's yard, then continues across the fields.

Go over a footbridge and along the farm track to reach a wooded area. Carry on to cross the railway again, then turn right to follow a quiet lane that becomes Meadow Road. When this meets Wansford Road turn right to walk along Anderson Street and Riverhead back to the start.

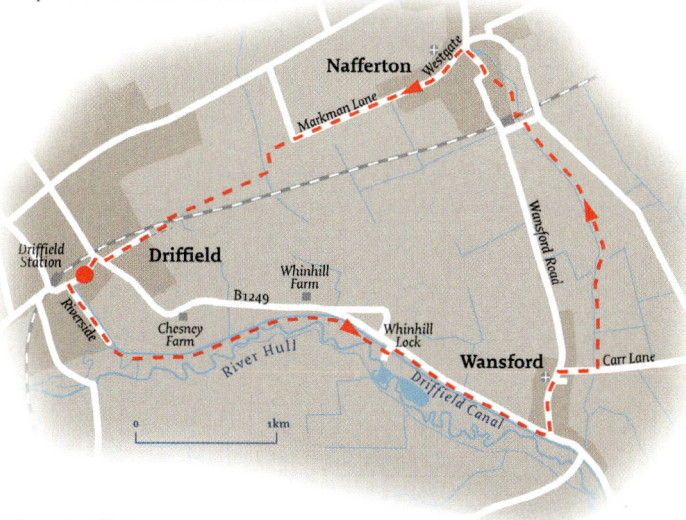

◀ Riverhead in Driffield

# Foston on the Wolds

**Distance** 3.5km **Time** 1 hour
**Terrain** tracks and pavement
**Map** OS Explorer 292 **Access** limited buses to Foston on the Wolds from Driffield

**This walk starts unusually by going through a door in Foston on the Wolds, a bucolic village south of Bridlington, and continues over gentle farmland and along a rare chalk stream.**

The walk starts from St Andrew's Church in the single-road village established to take advantage of the waters of nearby Foston Beck. A grain mill and three fulling mills operated here before industrialisation. 'Fulling' is a step in woollen cloth making that removes lanolin and shrinks the wool.

Look for the signpost pointing to a wooden door opposite the church noticeboard. Although it looks as though it will open into a garden, the door actually leads to a path which goes between houses and across a field. Go through a farm gate and turn right to follow a path alongside a drain. Over the centuries many streams and drains have been straightened and redirected to help relieve flooding in this area.

Turn left at a footpath sign to follow the hedge and enjoy the wide-ranging views. When this path meets a track, turn left to follow it alongside Foston Beck, one of the most northerly continuous chalk streams in the world and a very rare environment recognised as part of the River Hull SSSI (Site of Special Scientific

Interest). These clear, mineral-rich streams are known as the 'English rain forest'; of the 210 rivers classed as chalk streams globally, 160 are in England. Excessive abstraction of chalk streams by private water companies, however, has led to many streams drying up, causing great ecological damage.

At the bridge, cross sides to continue following the beck and at the road turn right, then left to follow a footpath through the farmyard of Mill Farm. The old mill here was once at the cutting edge of flour mill technology; it is thought to be one of only 11 mills in the country that used both water and steam power, and was one of only four to have rollers installed which produced a higher-quality white flour than that milled using traditional stones.

Continue past Brewery Farm onto Mill Lane to meet the main road, then cross over to follow the footpath back into the village to return to the start.

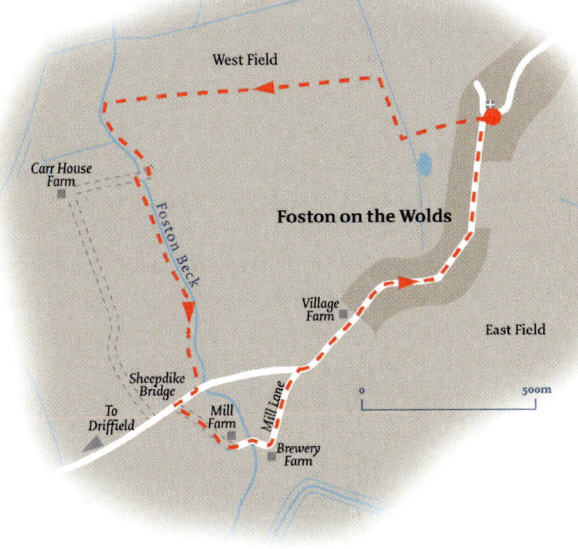

◀ Foston Beck

# Hornsea Mere

**Distance** 9.5km **Time** 3 hours
**Terrain** country roads, tracks and paths
**Map** OS Explorer 292 **Access** buses from Hull, Beverley and Bridlington stop by the access road to Hornsea Mere

Only 1km from the sea, the freshwater lake of Hornsea Mere is a popular spot for rowing, sailing, fishing and birdwatching. This walk goes along one side of the mere, by far the largest in Yorkshire, and returns along the old Hornsea to Hull railway line.

Start the walk from the car park at the sailing club on Kirkholme Point where there is plenty of parking. Walk back along the access road and turn right on the B1242 road to Hull. At the roundabout turn right again on Hull Road and continue along the pavement. Once past the last house on the right, look out for a metal gate and information boards in a field. Go through the gate and follow the path across the field on the south side of the mere.

The shallow lake was formed at the end of the last ice age on a bed of boulder clay surrounded by undulating deposits of gravel which trapped the water. Now a popular place for watersports, it was a base for RNAS (Royal Naval Air Service) seaplanes during the First World War and the brick buildings from that time are still in use today by the boatyard and café. Keen birdwatchers should look out for

# Hornsea Mere

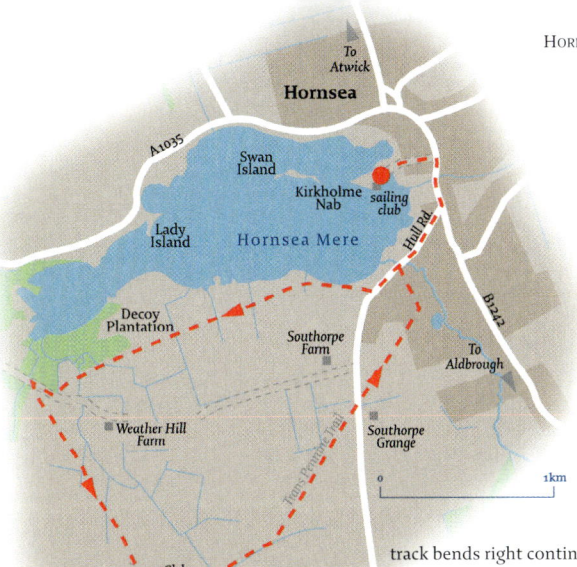

gulls, wildfowl and swifts in summer, as well as rarer grebes and ducks.

Continue across fields, passing through four further gates to arrive at a wooden footbridge into the next field; cross the field to another gate. Once through this gate, turn right for a few steps until you see a metal gate located slightly uphill, further along the hedge. Go through this, then turn left to follow the footpath across the field. Exit the field through a green metal gate in the far corner, then cross another field aiming for the buildings and wind turbines.

The path joins a vehicle track and as the track bends right continue ahead, aiming towards St Giles Church. This is one of the very few Georgian churches in East Yorkshire and although isolated is still in occasional use. Follow the path around the church, then turn left onto the road until you pass the last house on the left. At this point look for a footpath sign by the hedge and follow the path around the garden, then along the edge of the field to a wooden bridge into another field.

Continue on the path alongside a drainage ditch until the path crosses over the ditch and joins the bed of the old railway line. Follow this towards Hornsey, passing under Hull Road and continuing to a T-junction. Turn left to leave the old railway line and pass between allotments to rejoin Hull Road and turn right to return to the start.

**The River Derwent** is the western boundary for most of the walks in this chapter which are all within reach of the popular and well-connected market towns of Malton and Pocklington, both welcoming gateways for those walking the Wolds.

As the river flows from north to south it has historically been a barrier to east-west travel, especially between York and the coast. Malton, therefore, owes its development to its location at a vital crossing point which was first bridged during the Roman occupation. On the other side of the water is the twin town of Norton-on-Derwent which also features in the walks in this chapter.

Not far away, the small, peaceful villages of Wintringham, Thixendale, Settrington, Huggate and Millington are the starting points for routes through typical Wolds landscapes of undulating farmland bisected by dry steep-sided valleys. The western Wolds can be more heavily wooded in places, however, and there are other pleasant surprises, such as the artworks found on the walk from Wintringham, the beautiful riverside ruins at Kirkham and the famous deserted village of Wharram Percy.

On the other side of the Derwent there is a tour of the grand gardens and Baroque follies of the Castle Howard estate with views of the Howardian Hills.

# The Derwent and the Western Wolds

1. **Wintringham and Knapton Brow** 54
   Climb up to a high viewpoint and enjoy some cultural heritage

2. **Settrington Beacon** 56
   Follow in the footsteps of the Romans through woodlands and across fields

3. **Malton Old Town** 58
   Wander the historic streets of the bustling market town and return along a peaceful riverside path

4. **Norton and the Derwent** 60
   Trot through paddocks and fields before following the Derwent back to town

5. **Castle Howard loop** 62
   Take the tour of one of England's finest grand estates packed with glorious architectural statements and curiosities

6. **Kirkham Priory** 64
   Walk the riverside path and explore some enigmatic ecclesiastical ruins

7. **Wharram Percy** 66
   Trace the outlines of past lives and a lost rural community

8. **Thixendale** 68
   Start from an estate village to climb through some wonderful Wolds scenery

9. **Huggate** 70
   Take a breather on one of the Wolds Way poetry benches found on this circuit of idyllic dales

10. **Millington and Sylvan Dale** 72
    Look out for markers of Bronze Age and Roman occupation on this circuit of steep-sided valleys

# Wintringham and Knapton Brow

**Distance** 5km **Time** 1 hour 40
**Terrain** country roads, tracks and paths; short steep section **Map** OS Explorer 300
**Access** no public transport to the start

This walk takes in the steepest section of the Wolds Way, a short-lived but stiff climb in an otherwise serene and gently rolling landscape. The reward for your efforts is an artwork celebrating the ancient cultural landscape of the area and panoramic views over the Vale of Pickering from Knapton Brow.

Start the walk from the parking lay-by opposite St Peter's Church in the small village of Wintringham, just off the A64 east of Malton. This beautiful Norman church with Jacobean pews and medieval carvings sometimes offers refreshments for weary travellers and is well worth exploring. From the church, go to the bend in the road and follow the path straight ahead to climb along the edge of the field to meet a forestry track.

Turn left to follow the track around the edge of the plantation until it begins to bend sharply left. At this point continue ahead to climb very steeply up Deep Dale with a rope handrail to assist if needed. After passing through a hand-carved gate, and catching your breath on Knapton Brow, you can explore *Enclosure Rites*, an artwork by Jony Easterby.

A chalk path with split oak posts leads to a viewing platform overlooking a circular 'sky mirror' dew pond. Water is a constant challenge in the Wolds given the porous nature of chalk and these ponds

were once a common way of making sure farm animals had water. They were made by creating a depression, then lining it with non-porous clay or lime. While the artwork was being installed, real Bronze Age barrows were uncovered and these are still visible as indentations just to the north. The wooden carved *Guardian Warriors* are based on small Iron Age carved chalk figures made by Parisi tribespeople which were found in the Derwent Valley.

From the artwork descend along a very old sunken lane with views of the North York Moors in good weather. At the single-track road, turn left, then quickly right to follow the Wolds Way along the top edge of Knapton Plantation, then continue along the track until you see a path off to the right. Head towards the Wolds Way Caravan and Camping site, using the mast for orientation, then turn right onto the track along its edge. Carry on along the road and look out for the sunken lane followed earlier. From here, return the way you came, taking care going down the steep slope of Deep Dale.

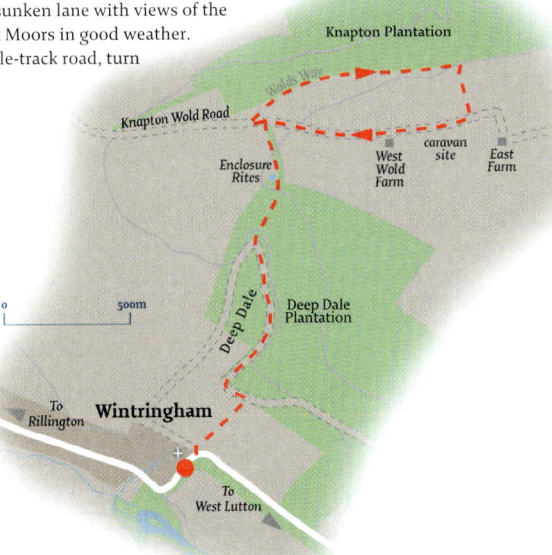

◀ The *Guardian Warriors*

# Settrington Beacon

**Distance** 11km **Time** 3 hours 40
**Terrain** country roads and tracks
**Map** OS Explorer 300 **Access** buses from Malton to Settrington

This more demanding walk crosses some of the highest ground in the area and takes in the site of a Roman signal beacon around 200m above sea level which received signals from a fire in the grounds of the present Scarborough Castle and relayed them to York.

Start the walk from the junction opposite the primary school in the village of Settrington, just east of Malton. Limited parking can be found along Back Lane or near the chapel. Walk along Back Lane until it leaves the village and at the road junction turn left to follow the signs to Settrington House. The road begins to climb a steep hill, offering great views of the house; continue along the road until you see the dirt track for Wardale House.

The gradient eases and views begin to develop with a Bronze Age tumuli visible across the valley. When the track turns towards the house continue straight ahead to go through a wooden farm gate into a field and contour left beside a wood. At the far end of the trees walk straight ahead towards the pond and go through a gate, then climb through the next field to another wooden gate. Ignore the vehicle tracks ahead to follow a faint footpath off to the left, aiming for the left of the house to reach a stile.

Once over the stile, turn left to follow the drive and cross a road, then follow the

◂ The modern beacon above Settrington

footpath sign straight across the field. This leads to another sign for a footpath that descends alongside a hedge and then skirts the wonderfully named ruin of Many Thorns Farm. Behind it, a track leads into the woods.

Go through the metal gate and down the slope to follow the path until you reach a Wolds Way sign. Turn right to climb back into woods and go through the gate to follow the signposted track as it meanders to a trig point and water tower.

An iron brazier beacon stood here on the High Street ridge during the Roman occupation ready to receive news from the coast of invasion from across the North Sea. A more modern version lit for national celebrations is nearby.

Leave the woods, then turn right and cross the road to a further path, signposted for High Bellmanear. Continue along the track until you reach a fingerpost for a footpath off to the right. Follow this down through fields and a small wood to then trend left towards the buildings of Low Bellmanear. Once at the house turn right to follow the meandering drive away from the house back to the road into Settrington.

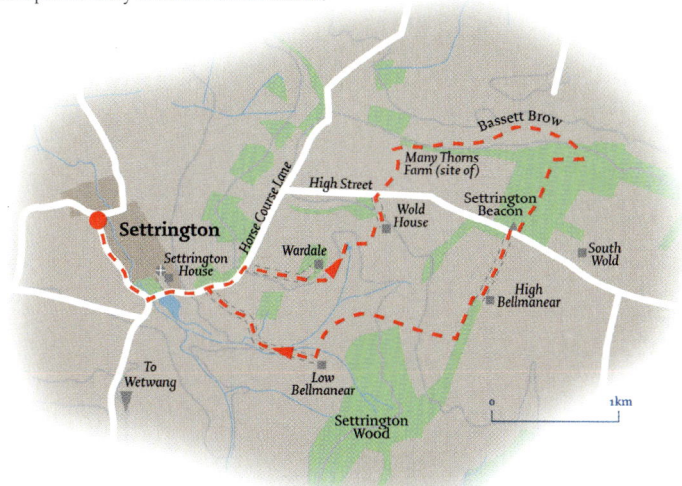

# Malton Old Town

**Distance** 5.5km **Time** 1 hour 45
**Terrain** country roads, tracks and paths
**Map** OS Explorer 300 **Access** buses and trains from York, Filey, Bridlington and Driffield to Malton

The attractive old market town of Malton was founded around the year 70AD when the Roman fort of Derventio Brigantum was built here at a crossing of the Derwent. The surrounding settlement grew and prospered as a commercial centre, especially during the Victorian and Edwardian eras, and remains a popular hub for visitors to the area, known for its vibrant independent shops, local artisan producers, food markets and festivals. This walk explores the older parts of town before returning along the river.

Start from the railway station and walk along Railway Street to cross the river and reach Yorkersgate. Turn left, then right by the Palace Cinema into Chancery Lane where you'll find the former offices of Charles Smithson, a lifelong friend of Charles Dickens and the inspiration for the character of Spenlow in *David Copperfield*. Like the fictional Spenlow, Smithson died without leaving a will, a major oversight for a solicitor. The office is also said to have been the template for Ebenezer Scrooge's barren workplace in *A Christmas Carol*.

Continue to Market Place and go around the town hall, the former butter market, to join Finkle Street and follow it downhill before turning right onto

Newbiggin. Continue along Newbiggin as it becomes Wheelgate and at the crossroads turn left for Old Malton. Continue along this road, passing the rugby ground, and after the Old Malton sign look out for St Mary's Priory Church, the only surviving building of a site founded in 1131 by the Gilbertine Order.

Continue to a car park and turn right to follow the path to the river which is followed back to Malton. Meander through Lady Spring Wood, enjoying the wildlife as you go, then pass between the brick pillars of the old railway bridge and turn right to go up some steps and enter Orchard Fields. Walk uphill to the stone monument, a marker for the Roman fort that was established to guard the north bank of the river during the first phase of the military occupation of Yorkshire. Malton Museum (found back on Yorkersgate near the cinema) displays many of the Roman artefacts found here.

Go back down the field over the old lines of defence, and exit near the fire station. Follow the road to a junction, then continue ahead on Castlegate to reach the crossroads from earlier. Turn left onto Yorkersgate then left onto Railway Street to return to the station.

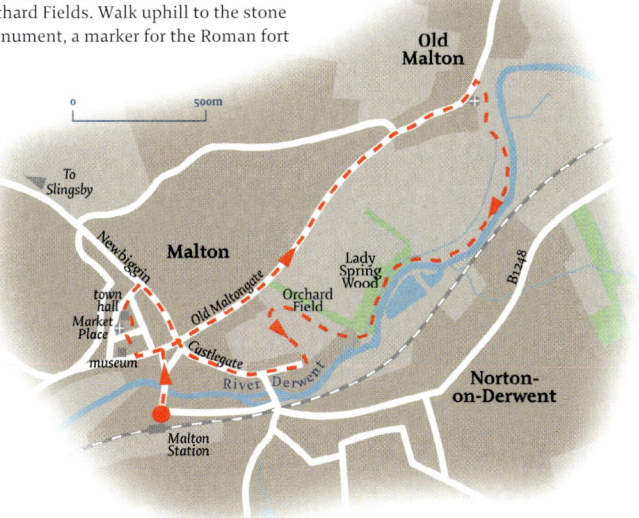

◀ St Michael's, Malton

# Norton and the Derwent

**Distance** 10.5km **Time** 3 hours
**Terrain** country roads, tracks and paths
**Map** OS Explorer 300 **Access** buses and trains from York, Filey, Bridlington and Driffield to Malton

Norton-on-Derwent, or more usually just Norton, is separated from Malton by the river and together the two towns are known as one of the principal centres in the country for the horse-racing industry, with many stables in and around the town. This circuit goes through horse paddocks, farmland and a golf course before returning along the River Derwent. The riverside path goes through the floodplain and can get muddy; do not attempt the walk when the water is running high or is in flood. Always stay well clear of horses and young foals in the fields and keep dogs on a lead.

Start from Malton railway station and go along Norton Road to the level crossing, then right on Welham Road away from town. Look out for The Avenue, a private road off to the right, and take the footpath left off it. Follow this between houses to emerge at a track, then use the stiles to cross between fields. Exit in the far corner and then go around the gallops.

Norton and Malton together are often referred to as the 'Newmarket of the North' as the good drainage and varied gradients of the local wolds make it ideal for training racehorses. The first race meeting in the area was held in 1692 at Langton Wold, just to the south of Norton. The 'sport of kings' took off around then following the restoration of Charles II; under the puritan leadership of Oliver Cromwell horse racing and

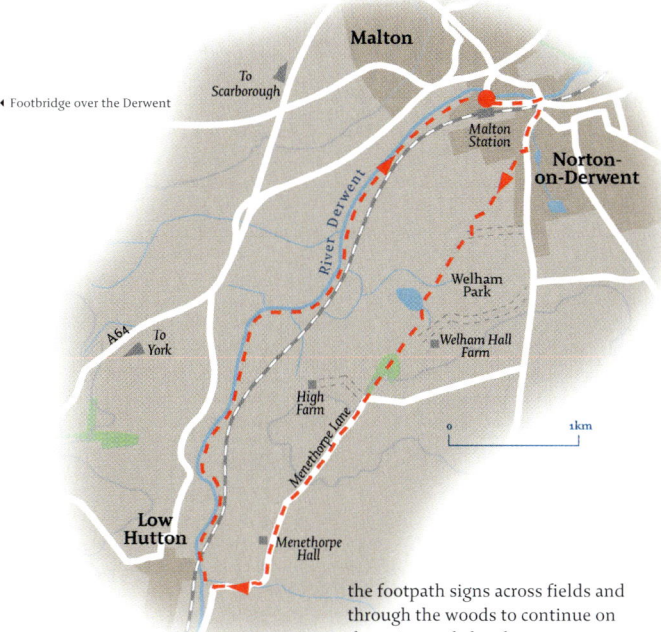

◂ Footbridge over the Derwent

gambling had been banned. The area's racing scene peaked in the mid-1800s as the railways brought spectators and big prizes; disaster struck in 1862, however, when commonland where regular races were held was divided up and sold off under the Enclosure Acts.

Enter the yard by the stile and cross over to continue between hedges to arrive at the entrance to the golf club. Keep going straight all the way through the fairways on the tarmac track to exit at a bridge over an ornamental lake. On the far side turn right to cross a stile and follow the footpath signs across fields and through the woods to continue on the quiet road ahead.

When the road nears the River Derwent, take the path off into the trees on the right to follow a footpath, part of the Centenary Way. Don't cross the attractive steel suspension footbridge which was built by the London and North Eastern Railway Company to allow access to the old station for Huttons Ambo which served Low and High Hutton (Ambo is Latin for 'both'). Instead, continue between the railway line and the river back to Norton. The path eventually emerges on Riverside View which leads back to the railway station.

# Castle Howard loop

**Distance** 8km **Time** 2 hours 30
**Terrain** country roads, tracks and paths
**Map** OS Explorer 300 **Access** buses from York and Malton to Castle Howard

**Alongside Blenheim, Chatsworth and Longleat, the magnificent Castle Howard is one of England's great country houses. This well-signposted walk around the edge of the estate has views of striking follies, landscaped parkland and the beautiful rolling Howardian Hills, as well as glimpses of the Howard family's Baroque masterpiece at its centre.**

Start from the exit of the car park (free) near the roundabout and the Ripon Obelisk. From the roundabout walk between the lime trees and the road towards Slingsby. The path crosses the clay-lined Obelisk Ponds and continues between the road and the estate boundary.

At the crossroads marked by a pair of ornate gateposts and a gatehouse, turn right to walk through the estate houses of Coneysthorpe with its village green and Georgian chapel. Once through the village look out for white wooden gates to the right; turn here to join a gravel track that is signposted for Welburn.

Enjoy views of the great house as you follow the signs to Bog Hall on the Centenary Way. After passing the buildings and continuing around, look out for the Temple of the Four Winds sitting on the skyline at the edge of Ray Wood. Designed by John Vanbrugh, the principal architect of Castle Howard as

well as Blenheim Palace, the temple was intended as a place for leisurely reading with a cellar below for servants to prepare food and drinks. The folly featured several times in the 1980s TV series *Brideshead Revisited*, one of many productions filmed around the estate.

Continue along the track and as the temple fades the huge Howard family mausoleum hoves into view on a mound. Designed by Vanburgh's assistant, Nicholas Hawksmoor, it is one of the largest mausoleums in Europe; the vaulted burial vault contains 63 catacombs.

Keep on along the track until it reaches a T-junction at Low Gaterley and turn right to continue along the Centenary Way. As progress is made a limestone pyramid appears off to the left. Aligned with Castle Howard, this was used as a viewing point and 'eye-catcher'. Continue along the track until you reach the imposing Pyramid Gatehouse where you turn right to follow a path between the trees and the road back to the start.

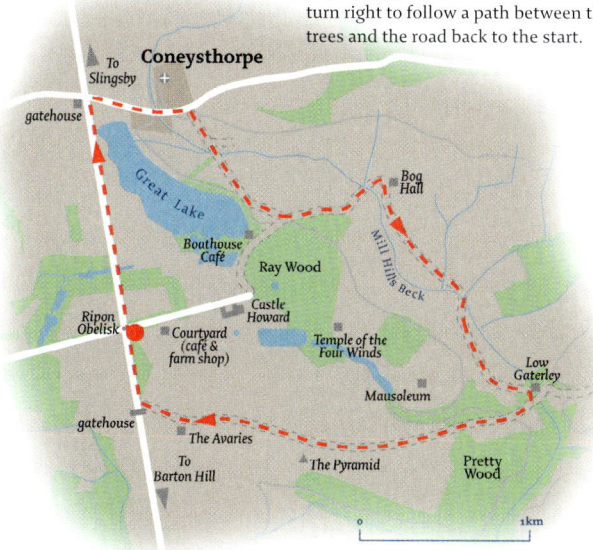

◀ Castle Howard Mausoleum and New River Bridge

# Kirkham Priory

**Distance** 7.5km **Time** 2 hours 15
**Terrain** country roads, tracks and paths
**Map** OS Explorer 300 **Access** buses from Malton stop on the A64 at Whitwell-on-the-Hill, a short walk from the priory

The riverside ruins of the 12th-century Augustinian priory at Kirkham are the starting point for this walk of two halves in the Derwent Valley. After a short sharp climb through woodland and across farmland, the return is an easy stroll along the bank of the wide River Derwent.

Start from the English Heritage car park (free) next to Kirkham Priory, just off the A64 York road south of Malton. Cross the fine stone bridge which connects the North and East Ridings of Yorkshire and continue over the York to Scarborough railway line, passing the surviving 1856 brick signal box. Look out for the walker's signpost by the side of the road and turn left into the woodland.

Walk up the steep track through Oak Cliff Wood to emerge at the top onto a road. After catching your breath and enjoying the views, turn left for a few steps, then go left again through the farm gate to return to the woods.

The path goes along the edge of the woods, then crosses a field to arrive at the access track for the picturesque Oakcliffe Farm. Follow the track to join Riders Lane and turn left to eventually cross the railway line again. Once past a couple of houses, look out for a footpath sign in a small copse of trees

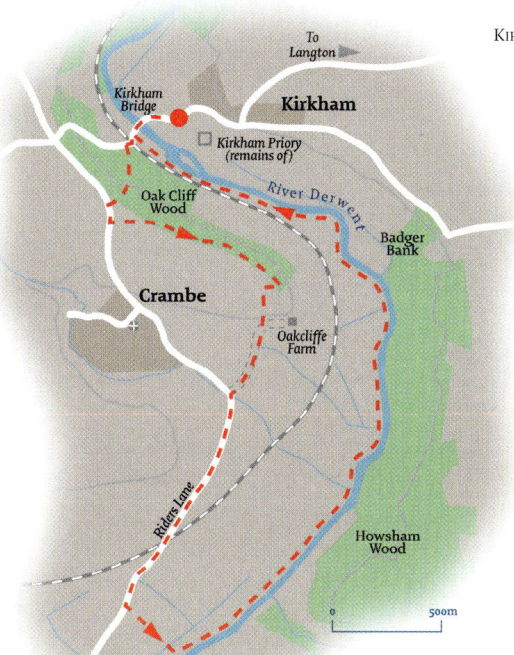

and go across the fields and a footbridge to reach the river.

From here it's an easy meander back to Kirkham Priory along the riverbank with only wildflowers and perhaps a heron or kingfisher for company. As the end of the walk approaches there are good views of the ruined cloisters, refectory and kitchen of the priory. The priory was surrendered in 1539 during the Dissolution of the Monasteries, one of more than 900 religious houses disbanded, seized and disposed of by Henry VIII.

The priory had been founded around 1122 by Walter l'Espec, Lord of Helmsley, who also built Rievaulx Abbey. The later Gothic gatehouse is especially interesting, with sculptures of St George and the Dragon and David and Goliath, as well as the armorials of various noble families.

Remarkably, the site was used in preparations for the D-Day landings on the beaches of Normandy in June 1944. The western cloister was covered in scrambling nets by men of the British 11th armoured division to simulate how they would get between their transport ships and smaller landing craft. Winston Churchill and King George VI visited in secret to oversee the training.

◀ The ruined gatehouse of Kirkham Priory

THE DERWENT AND THE WESTERN WOLDS

# Wharram Percy

**Distance** 6.5km **Time** 2 hours
**Terrain** country roads, tracks and field paths **Map** OS Explorer 300 **Access** no public transport to the start; buses from Malton stop at Wharram-le-Street

Wharram Percy is one of the most well-known and studied lost villages in England. Thought to have been settled in the Iron Age, the settlement in Deep Dale south of Wharram-le-Street was abandoned around 1500, a casualty of land clearance and the replacement of arable crops with sheep farming. This walk follows an old railway line into the dale before touring the deserted village.

Start from the English Heritage visitor car park south of Wharram-le-Street, off the B1248 Beverley to Malton road. Walk along the road past Bella Farm to a sharp right turn and follow the Wolds Way footpath along the edge of a field, enjoying views to the north and towards Malton. At the end of the track turn left onto Station Road to follow the Centenary Way. This quiet road descends to Station Cottage, where you turn left on the line of the old railway from Malton to Driffield along the bottom of the dale.

Some buildings connected with the railway are still visible, including the silo used to load trains with product from the old chalk quarry located nearby. The quarry is now the nature reserve passed on the way. Turn right where a bridge crosses the line and go through a gate to enter the Wharram Percy site.

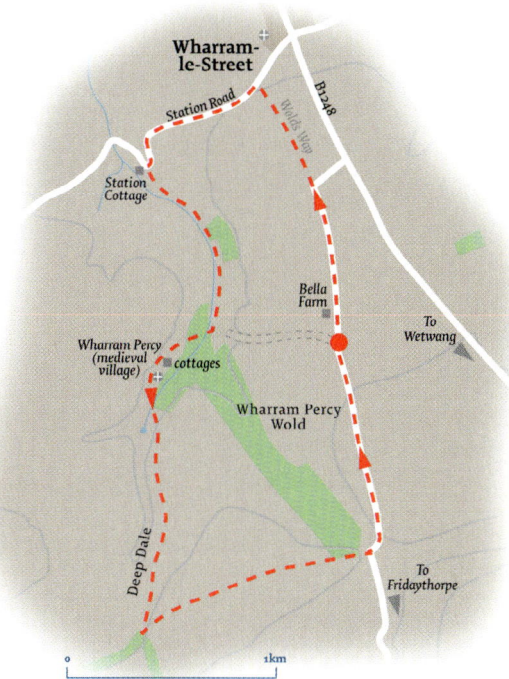

Continue past the cottages, which were part of a late 18th-century farmyard, to explore the atmospheric ruin of St Martins, the only medieval building left standing. The size and structure of the church changed several times over the years as the community around it grew and contracted. It survived longer than the rest of the buildings because it also served four neighbouring villages, of which only Thixendale survives today. The outlines of many lost houses can be seen on the grassy plateau above the remains of the church.

Leave Wharram Percy by walking past the old millpond and carrying on to the top edge of Deep Dale. When the dale bends right go through a farm gate with the Wolds Way to soon meet a road and turn left to follow the road back to the car park, enjoying the views as they open out.

◀ Ruin of St Martins, Wharram Percy

# Thixendale

**Distance** 6.5km **Time** 2 hours
**Terrain** country roads, tracks and paths
**Map** OS Explorer 300 **Access** seasonal bus service (Wolds Explorer) from Pocklington stops at Thixendale (weekends and bank holidays only)

Thixendale is a pretty, single-road settlement with a church, pub and cricket pitch nestled in the steep-sided Water Dale and surrounded by gently rolling hills. This walk goes through a typical Wolds landscape of steep-sided dry valleys, crossing earthwork evidence of the Bronze Age occupation of these dales.

Start from the Church of St Mary in Thixendale (limited parking nearby) off the A166 between Wetwang and Stamford Bridge. To the right of the church is the old spired village schoolhouse; both were built by the industrious Victorian agricultural improver Sir Tatton Sykes who also replaced thatched chalk cottages with brick houses during his time as owner of the Sledmere Estate. Without his intervention it is very likely that Thixendale would have perished like Wharram Percy and many other surrounding settlements.

Continue through the village to branch off left on the signposted Centenary Way, passing the village pub and going between the cricket field and pavilion. Carry on across the field and over a stile into the next field. After joining the track near a white gate, go up the side of the valley along the hedge to the top. This part of the route offers great views across the area. Keep with the path as it bends to the right, go through a gate and follow another hedge to join a track. Follow the Centenary Way left at a wooden fence, then turn left to join the Wolds Way on a track.

Turn left at the next crossroads to follow the Wolds Way onto a footpath through trees and down to a gate. Continue down into Cow Wold and through a further gate to follow the Wolds Way uphill to another gate. Turn right here to climb steeply, then meander left and right to go through some more trees.

Once out of the woodland, the track descends into the village offering a great view down into Thixendale. Said to be the last place in the UK to get television reception and reliant for many years on its own small transmitter, it is not hard to see why when viewed from here.

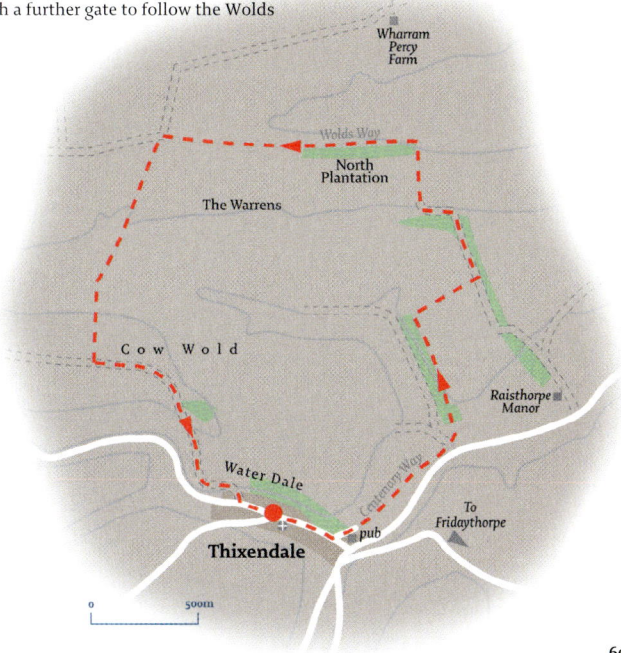

# Huggate

**Distance** 8km **Time** 2 hours 30
**Terrain** country roads, paths and tracks
**Map** OS Explorer 294 **Access** seasonal bus service (Wolds Explorer) from Pocklington stops at Huggate (weekends and bank holidays only)

Although it lies in a hollow, the little village of Huggate lays claim to being the highest in the Wolds at 170m above sea level. This walk tours some of the idyllic steep-sided dry chalk valleys which encircle it and for the most part follows well-signposted paths.

Start from Huggate's free car park on the edge of the village, just east of the crossroads on Driffield Road, and follow the signposted path. Pass the village green, site of one of the deepest wells in England which previously supplied the locals with water, and go right along the road. Keep on to leave the houses behind when the road becomes the sunken Town End Lane. Pass the access for Glebe Farm and keep going towards Northfield Farm before reaching a Wolds Way signpost. Follow this across the side of the field to a gate and bear right to reach a bench.

This is Horse Dale and the bench is one of the six 'poetry benches' found dotted along the Wolds Way. Designed by Angus Ross, the steam-bent oak represents the shape of the dales and the poem inscribed into it is by John Wedgwood Clarke. From the bench you can see Horse, Holm and Harper Dales and it is sited in the middle

of some Bronze Age earthworks.

Continue to follow the path as it gently leads down to the bottom of Horse Dale and reaches metal gates. Ignore the Wolds Way sign this time and take the route through the gate to the right. Follow the path along the bottom of this meandering dale, then climb to a cattle grid and farm gate at the right-hand end of the woodland.

Follow the farm track as it bends sharply right, then follow the footpath sign off to the left down into Rabbit Dale. At the bottom turn right to follow the path through a metal gate and continue along the meandering valley until you reach a wooden farm gate.

Join the Chalkland Way here and continue through Cow Dale to another gate to meet the outbound lane and return to the start.

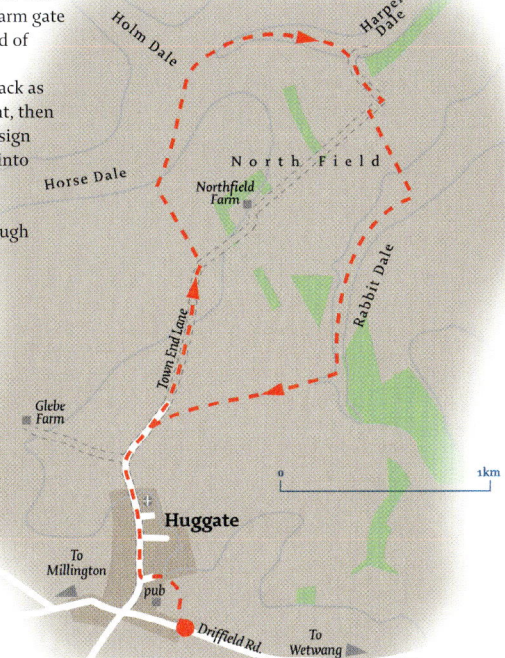

◀ Cow Dale

# Millington and Sylvan Dale

**Distance** 5km **Time** 2 hours 15
**Terrain** country roads, tracks and paths
**Map** OS Explorer 294 **Access** seasonal
bus service (Wolds Explorer) from
Pocklington stops at Millington
(weekends and bank holidays only)

**Surrounded by steep-sided dry valleys rich in wildlife and historical interest, the village of Millington is a popular walkers' hub. This circuit passes the only wooded dale in the Wolds and there are steep sections with climbs which are rewarded with excellent views.**

Start on Swineridge Lane at the top of Millington near St Margaret's Church and follow the crossroads sign towards Millington Pastures to leave the village. Follow the road as it climbs past Woodgate Farm to a hairpin bend where there are four hitching posts by the side of the road. These hitching posts are part of the Wolds Way sculpture trail; there are 11 of them in total and each has a letter which taken together spell out 'Gait in Wold'. A gait is an old measure of common grazing land before fencing was used, with one gait being enough for six sheep or four ewes with lambs.

Carry on around the bend past the access to Lily Dale and Millington Woods, a local nature reserve woodland with a surviving pocket of ancient ash trees, a remnant of a much larger wildwood.

Continue on the road to a signed footpath which drops down to cross the stream by a wooden footbridge. This is thought to be the route of a Roman road and there is evidence to suggest that there was a large camp nearby. Some historians

◂ Hitching posts on the Wolds Way sculpture trail

also suggest the settlement of Delgovicia or Delgovitia was located at the site of Millington, although there are several other candidates.

Continue along Sylvan Dale to another fingerpost and turn right to follow the Wolds Way uphill. Go through the gate, then along the edge of the field towards the access road for Warren Farm. Look out for undulations in the ground as you go; these are the Wold Entrenchments, marking boundaries from the Bronze Age or earlier which could have been used for defence, stock-herding or as a symbol of power.

At the farm, follow the Wolds Way to a wooden gate, then walk along the Minster Way down through a field until you reach the corner of a wire fence. From here follow the footpath and duckboards across Millington Beck back into the village. Turn left to return to the start.

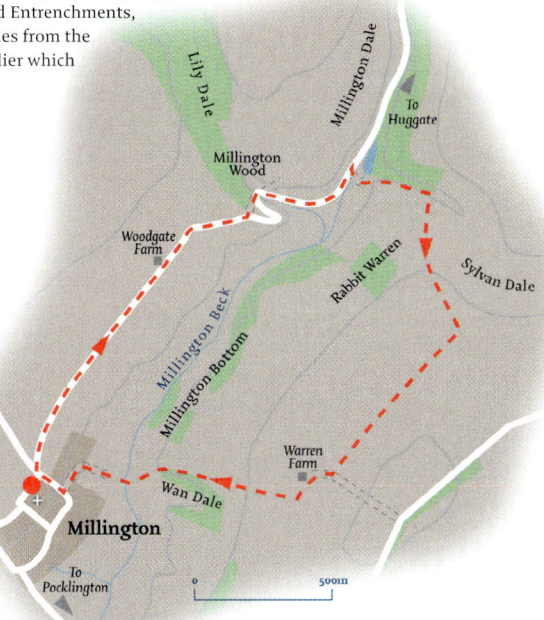

Beverley Minster ▶

**The gently rolling chalk** uplands of the southern Wolds sit between Beverley and the Humber Estuary to the south and Market Weighton to the north, and between the flat farmlands of the Humberhead Levels to the west and the Holderness Plain to the east. With gentler contours than other parts of the Wolds, the far-reaching views over peaceful countryside are easier to reach and water is never far away.

The characterful market towns of Pocklington and Market Weighton are well connected and good bases for exploring the area, but elegant Beverley is the cultural centre. As well as its spectacular Gothic church, genteel cobbled streets and busy market days, it still has a wonderful area of historic common grazing where cows wander freely in the summer.

Other walks in this chapter visit long-lost villages and manor houses, old Tudor deer parks and former railway lines now re-purposed for the enjoyment of walkers and cyclists. There are also walks around North Cave Wetlands and Kelsey Lakes, former quarries now restored as wildlife and recreation havens, and the chalk cliffs of 'Little Switzerland', a country park which overlooks the Humber.

# Southern Wolds and the Humber

**1** **Warter pilgrimage** 76
March in the footsteps of religious rebels through quiet countryside

**2** **Londesborough** 78
Tour a grand old estate which was once the stomping ground of diplomats, aristocrats and kings

**3** **Market Weighton** 80
Steam along the former railway line named after a disgraced Victorian 'Railway King'

**4** **Cherry Burton** 82
Roll pleasantly along the trackbed of the old Beverley to York railway line

**5** **Beverley and the Westwood** 84
Enjoy the historic curiosities found around the home town of one of England's greatest Gothic churches

**6** **Risby Park** 86
Take a trip back to Tudor times on this circuit of farmland, old deer park and long-lost mansions

**7** **North Cave Wetlands** 88
Ramble around a former industrial landscape now restored, rewilded and bursting with birdlife

**8** **Drewton Dale and St Austin's Stone** 90
Hike up through a dale known for old tales of preachers and druids

**9** **Hessle and Little Switzerland** 92
Wander away from the water's edge to explore an historic country park with chalk cliffs and great views

**10** **Kelsey Lakes** 94
Follow ditches and drains on this wildlife-packed wetland safari

# Warter pilgrimage

**Distance** 11km **Time** 3 hours 30
**Terrain** country roads, tracks and fields
**Map** OS Explorer 294 **Access** no public transport to the start

**The Pilgrimage of Grace was a rebellion by English Catholics in the north against Henry VIII's break with the Church in Rome in 1536 and the promotion of 'base-born' Thomas Cromwell as his enforcer. This route from the attractive village of Warter, which once had a monastic priory, follows part of the route taken by many of the rebels as they made their way from Market Weighton to congregate in York and petition their king.**

Start from the war memorial in Warter and walk along the Nunburnholme road (where there is a large free car park). Pass the primary school, then go left at the T-junction and continue across a stream and past Methill Hall Farm along Back Lane. This lane eventually meets the road which goes through the village of Nunburnholme, the site of a long-gone 12th-century Benedictine priory.

For many communities in England who suffered during poor harvests, these buildings not only provided religious instruction but also shelter and charity. When both of the priories at Warter and Nunburnholme were dissolved on the same day in October 1536 on the order of Cromwell, there was understandably great anger and dismay. A few days before, Robert Aske, a London barrister from Selby, gathered supporters in Market

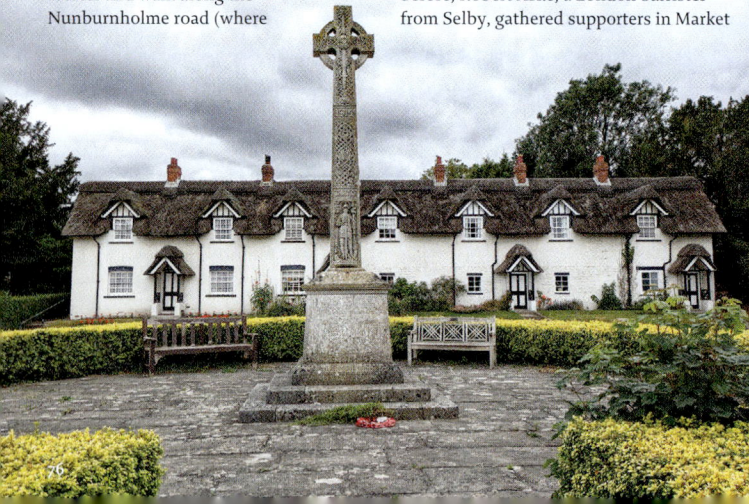

Weighton and set off to march on York via the two religious houses. Aske eventually met the king in London but, after initially agreeing to many of the insurgents' demands, he changed his mind and had the rebel leaders charged with high treason. Aske was tried in Westminster and hung in chains at York before being executed at Clifford's Tower.

Follow the road through the village to the red telephone box and look for a Wolds Way signpost. Leave the historic rebels' route here to cross the farmyard and go over a wooden footbridge. Continue uphill through gates and fields, then go right between the fence and hedge, and carry on to reach another farmyard at Partridge Hall. Follow the signs through this and along the access track to the road.

Turn left on the road and climb past a quarry and straight on at the crossroads, then look out for a bridleway sign at the next farm. Follow this down into Nunburnholme Wold and skirt the woodland to rejoin Back Lane, then turn right to retrace your steps back to Warter.

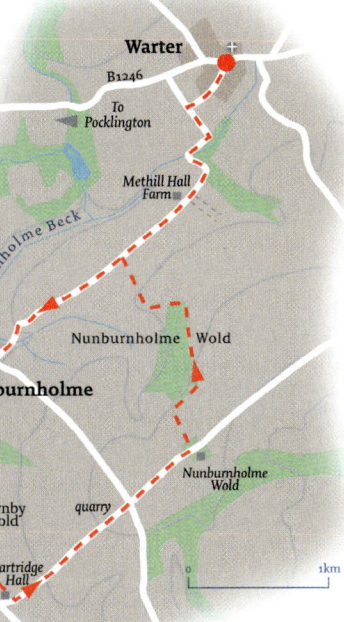

◀ War memorial in Warter village centre

# Londesborough

**Distance** 3.5km **Time** 1 hour
**Terrain** country lanes and tracks
**Map** OS Explorer 294 **Access** buses to Londesborough from York, Pocklington and Beverley

**A grand country estate with a colourful history just north of Market Weighton is the setting for this short walk around ponds and peaceful parkland.**

Start from outside All Saints Church on Low Street in the estate village of Londesborough. The Norman church has some interesting features and is thought to have been built on the site of a pagan temple. According to legend, King Edwin converted to Christianity here in 626.

Walk past the churchyard and the metal gates of 'The Wilderness', the garden that was developed with the first grand house in the 18th century. Continue to the end of the road and, with the entrance to Londesborough Hall ahead, go right on the signposted Wolds Way.

The estate was established by the Clifford family, the Earls of Cumberland, in the 16th and 17th centuries. The original 70-room hall was demolished in 1819, however, by the 6th Duke of Devonshire who couldn't afford the upkeep while reconstructing his other property, Chatsworth House in Derbyshire. In its place he built a 'Shooting Box', a smaller hunting lodge on the site of the present house.

The estate was later bought by George Hudson, a railway financier known as the 'Railway King', who built his own railway station in the grounds but fled the country to avoid prison after defrauding

◀ The lake at Londesborough

his investors. The next owner was Albert Denison, a politician and diplomat who built most of the present house, restored the gardens and hosted Edward VII and George V on the estate.

Go through the woods and emerge between two pillars, then follow the vehicle track into the field. After around 50m, turn left to follow the footpath signs down through the field to the ornamental pond. Continue along the path to a road and turn left to follow it towards Easthorpe Farm. Old Easthorpe village no longer exists; it was cleared away to improve the view from the house in the 1730s.

As the track gently bends to the right look out for a footpath sign and go across the field, aiming for the end of the copse that can be seen ahead. Cross the footbridge and continue uphill through the fields and signposted gates, following a faint path. Arriving back at the ornate gates, retrace your steps back through the woodland to the start.

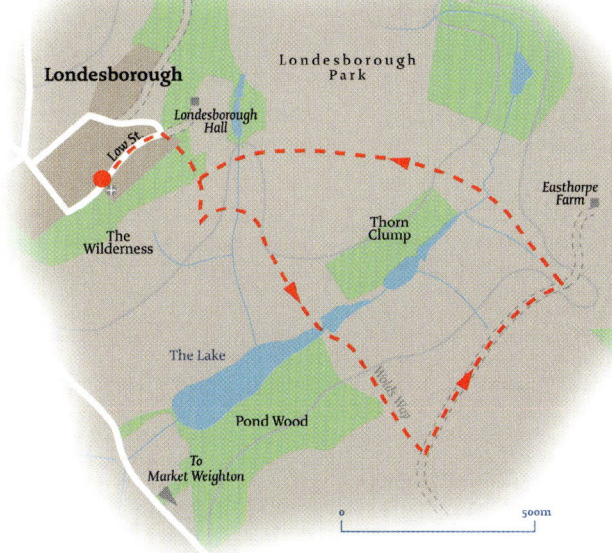

# Market Weighton

**Distance** 6km **Time** 2 hours
**Terrain** country roads, tracks and paths
**Map** OS Landranger 106 **Access** buses to Market Weighton from York, Pocklington, Beverley and Hull

As the name suggests, Market Weighton is an old market town and from 1847 to 1965 it was connected to York and Beverley by a railway line named after the Victorian 'Railway King', George Hudson. This walk follows part of the old line, now a 16km-long walking and cycling route, from Market Weighton before returning through Goodmanham, a village where a high priest is said to have ordered a pagan temple to be burnt down after his conversion to Christianity.

Start the walk from the free car park near Market Weighton's All Saints' Church on Londesborough Road. Go along Londesborough Road, past the public toilets, and turn onto Hall Road. Follow the Wolds Way footpath when this road bends left and continue on the tree-lined Hudson Way past the football pitches. The path follows the old railway line which carried mineral traffic through the North East, one of the many routes which made George Hudson's name. Although he did more than anyone to establish York as a great railway city by connecting Edinburgh and London through it, Hudson was forced to flee England and died in penury in 1871 after being found to have cheated many of his investors during the boom years.

This area is known as the Monkey Run; a 'monkey' is slang for 500 and the field here was once a holding area for that many sheep before they were sold at Market Weighton's sheep fairs. Keep on

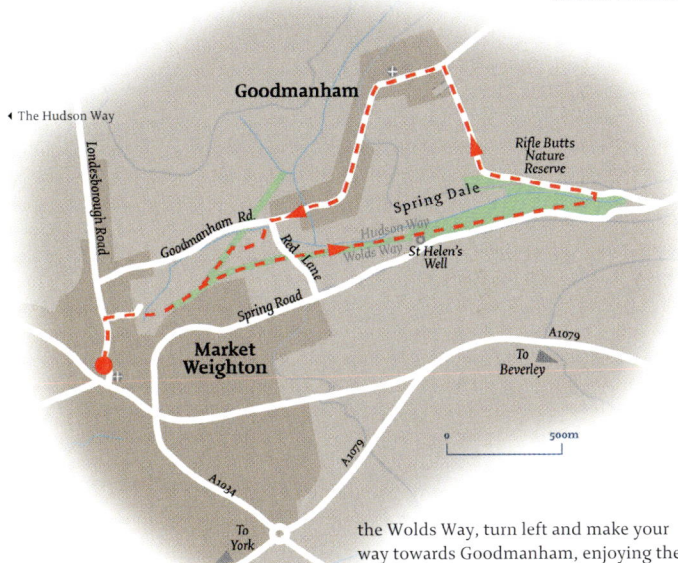

◀ The Hudson Way

along the Hudson Way to go under a bridge and soon arrive at peaceful St Helen's Well where water streams down through a natural grotto into a shallow bath. Being so close to the railway line, it also once provided refills for steam engines. The well water has reputed healing powers and is named after St Helena, the Christian mother of Constantius the Great who was proclaimed Emperor in York in 308AD.

Just before the Hudson Way reaches a country road you can take a break on one of the benches dotted along the Wolds Way, made by Angus Ross. This one features a poem by Scarborough-based John Clark. Once on the road that crosses the Wolds Way, turn left and make your way towards Goodmanham, enjoying the country views. Rifle Butts Quarry, a First World War rifle range that's now a nature reserve, can also be visited as you go.

Turn left at the junction outside the village and follow the Wolds Way to All Hallows' Church, said to be the site of a pagan temple set aflame by the high priest Coifi following King Edwin's enthusiastic embrace of the new religion sweeping the north in 627AD.

Ignore the Wolds Way signs from here as you continue through the village to the junction at Red Lane. Look out for a wooden kissing gate on the other side of the road, then make your way around the field and under a bridge to follow a wooded path back to the Hudson Way. Turn right to return to the start.

# Cherry Burton

**Distance** 5.5km **Time** 1 hour 45
**Terrain** country roads and tracks
**Map** OS Explorer 293 **Access** buses from Beverley to Cherry Burton

The village of Cherry Burton, northwest of Beverley, was once served by a railway line between Beverley and York. This walk follows an undulating section of the old line, now the Hudson Way walking and cycling route, before returning along the Wilberforce Way, named after the Hull-born abolitionist William Wilberforce.

Start from the pond in the picturesque village of Cherry Burton and head out of town on Main Street, passing the Church of St Michael and All Angels and the school. Once at the crossroads, turn right and walk alongside the road, then turn left on the signposted path just after Meadfoot House.

Follow the path by the drain to go over a bridge, then continue straight on to a gap in the hedge where you'll find some steps which lead up to the Hudson Way. Although named after the 'Railway King' George Hudson, this section of the line was built after the over-ambitious financier had fled the country, having been found to have cheated investors.

Turn left on the old railway line and continue under a roadbridge and past a picnic area to arrive at the old station for Cherry Burton, now a private house. Opened in 1865 by the North Eastern Railway, the station closed to passengers in 1959 following Dr Beeching's recommended cuts. Like many other rural stations, this one was oddly located away from the village it was supposed to serve.

Beyond the station, go down some steps and cross the road to rejoin the old

◂ Cherry Burton farmland

railway line. Once under the next roadbridge go up the ramp to the left and walk along Etton Road back to Cherry Burton. This part of the walk is on the Wilberforce Way, a 97km long-distance walking route between Hull and York via Pocklington, devised to mark the bicentenary of the abolition of the British Transatlantic Slave Trade in the 1807 Act of Parliament. The son of a wealthy merchant, William Wilberforce was born in Hull and the family house is now a museum there which is worth visiting. As well as displays of his journals and artefacts, there are items linked to the West African slave trade and its legacy.

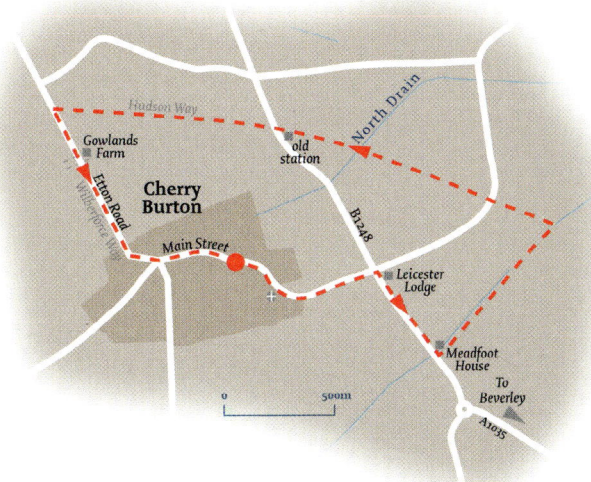

# Beverley and the Westwood

**Distance** 5.5km **Time** 1 hour 45
**Terrain** pavement and tracks
**Map** OS Explorer 293 **Access** buses to Beverley from Driffield, Hull and York; trains from York and Hull

This pleasant meander around the East Riding county town of Beverley crosses the heathland of the Westwood, historic grazing land controlled by the town's Pasture Masters. The ever-present Gothic masterpiece of Beverley Minster is a reminder of the market town's past as a significant wool-trading centre and place of pilgrimage in the Middle Ages.

Start from the clock in the square outside Beverley's railway station. Go along Trinity Lane and at the end turn left onto Eastgate, then right to pass in front of Beverley Minster and continue along Minster Moorgate.

Beverley owes its historic prominence as a religious centre to John of Beverley, a preacher who founded a monastery here around 700AD and was said to have miraculous healing powers. After being canonised in 1037, a cult developed around him and pilgrims flocked to Beverley, helping it to develop as a vibrant trading centre and in the 12th century work was begun on creating the magnificent Minster. With a soaring exterior and some of the finest stone carvings in England, it combines Early English, Perpendicular and Decorated periods of Gothic architecture and is larger than many cathedrals despite only being a parish church.

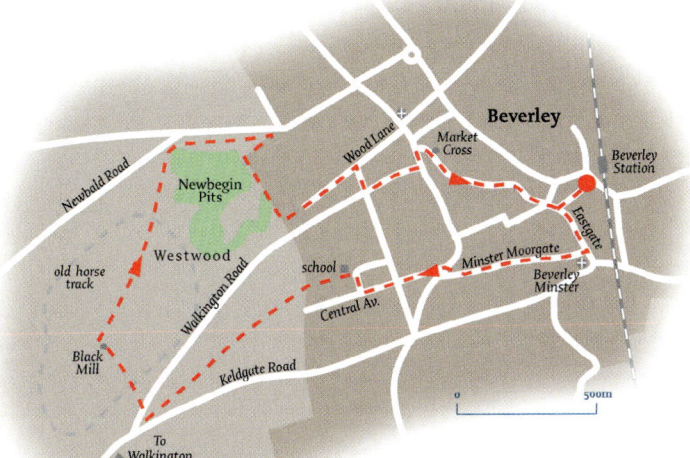

At the end of the road cross over the grass to join Central Avenue and continue along to Ellerker Road. Turn right onto this and take the tree-lined path left along the side of the school when the road bends right. Exit onto the Westwood and take a path to the left to walk across the grass to where the roads meet. Protected from enclosure since the 18th century, the Westwood is still used for cattle grazing in summer so dogs should be kept on a lead.

Near the far end, follow the path to the right to cross Walkington Road and continue towards the redundant Black Mill, an old wind-powered corn mill and landmark which sits alone on a small rise in the centre of the heath.

From the water trough beyond the mill, turn towards the far end of the old Tan Gallop, the town's first racecourse, with the Minster visible off to the right. Ignore the various paths that branch off to reach a parking area and, just beyond, double back on a concrete track which crosses a culvert then runs between houses and the woodland of Newbegin Pits, the site of old chalk pits also once used for cockfighting, ratting, bull-baiting and bareknuckle fighting.

Just before reaching the road, take a left turn to go through a metal gate and join a road. This bends right onto St Mary's Terrace, then left onto Newbegin. At the end of Newbegin turn left, then first right to arrive at the market square and the ornate market cross, known as the bandstand. From here, turn right to follow the road onto Eastgate, then go left onto Trinity Lane to return to the start.

◀ Black Mill on the Westwood

# Risby Park

**Distance** 4km **Time** 1 hour 15
**Terrain** country roads and tracks
**Map** OS Explorer 293 **Access** no public transport to the start

Risby Park is the site of a lost medieval country estate southwest of Beverley established by the Ellerker family, royal courtiers who once hosted deer hunts here for fellow Tudor nobles and Henry VIII himself. This gentle walk tours the old deer park and farmland, and passes the sites of two long-gone manor houses.

Start from the entrance to Risby Park Fishing Ponds, just off the A164 north of Cottingham. There is a good anglers' café on site with a view across the water to a ruined octagonal brick folly dating from the 1770s. From the gates, head along the road to the end of the woodland where a footpath takes you off along the trees to eventually meet a road at a sharp corner.

Cross and quickly re-cross the road, then follow the path along the edge of the field and through woodland to arrive at a noticeboard. This explains that the field to the north was once occupied by a long-gone moated Tudor manor house.

Cellar Heads was built by Sir Ralph Ellerker and his eldest son, soldiers in the court of Henry VIII, who were knighted after the rout of James IV's army at the Battle of Flodden in 1512. Despite supporting the failed Pilgrimage of Grace uprising in 1536, Sir Ralph was reprieved and died in his King's service during a siege in France. Beyond the house is a dry valley used as a deer course where

◀ Risby Folly

deer would be driven past a platform where waiting huntsmen stood ready to bring them down with bows and arrows.

Continue along the path, passing another woodland to join Park Lane close to Risby Park Farm. Turn left and follow this access track to eventually meet a road, then go left again to return to the start at the fishing ponds.

Along the way look out for indentations in the fields off to the left; these are the foundations of Risby Hall, a three-storey successor manor house to the one at Cellar Heads which burnt down in the late 1700s. Built in 1674 by Sir James Bradshaw, a descendant later established terraced gardens in front of the manor and dug the ornamental lakes, with a fashionable Romantic folly overlooking one of them.

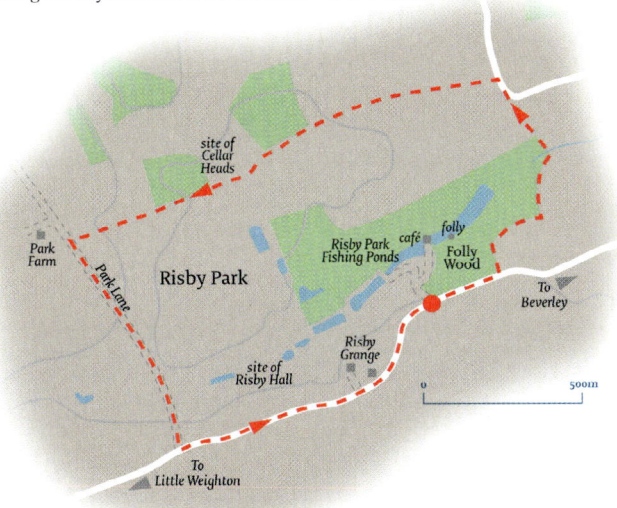

# North Cave Wetlands

**Distance** 9.5km **Time** 3 hours
**Terrain** country roads, farm tracks and paths **Map** OS Explorer 293 **Access** buses from Hull stop in North Cave

North Cave Wetlands is a remarkable example of an industrial landscape restored for the benefit of wildlife. The mixture of deep and shallow lakes with islands, grassy banks, reeds, meadows, hedges and woodland is home to avocets, buntings, sedge warblers, sand martins and gulls, with ducks and geese returning in the winter months. The area was once part of a huge marsh called Wallingfen and the site's ongoing restoration is managed by the Yorkshire Wildlife Trust.

Start from the junction of Dryham Lane and Cliffe Road near North Cave (free parking) and head along Dryham Lane to enjoy views over the wetlands created in worked-out sand and gravel quarries. In order to create the best possible habitat for resident and migrant birds the water levels of the lakes are carefully managed; lowered in summer to expose more bare ground for breeding and raised in winter to prevent vegetation taking over. As a result, more than 200 species of bird have been recorded on the reserve, as well as 24 species of butterfly and 18 of dragonfly.

When the ponds are replaced by farmland, pass a house and farm, and continue through the gates to meet a farm gate. Go through and cross the field to continue on the access track for Common Farm, then turn right on the track to South Carr Farm. Enjoy the views to the east over the Wolds, then cross a ditch and go around the side of the farm. When the track bends, head for the gate in the corner and follow the track that runs

◀ Looking out over North Cave Wetlands

alongside a drain towards North Carr Farm. Go right when you reach the road and carry on back along Carr Lane to Cliffe Road. Cross the busy road and continue up Common Hill to Hotham.

The village is named after Sir John Hotham, the proud governor of Hull who somehow managed to frustrate and betray both sides in the Civil War. Together with his equally duplicitous son, he was eventually executed on Tower Hill by order of Oliver Cromwell and afterwards called 'an notable monument of unprosperous disloyalty' by Charles I.

At the crossroads go straight ahead, then turn right at the war memorial onto Main Street. At a bend in the road keep ahead on a path between the houses to walk through the grounds of the Georgian Hotham Hall with the church tower of All Saints in North Cave in the distance. When the path meets a road, turn right and continue straight ahead to eventually return to the start.

Before you leave the wetlands it is well worth following the path to the Turret hide for one last grandstand view over the man-made wilderness.

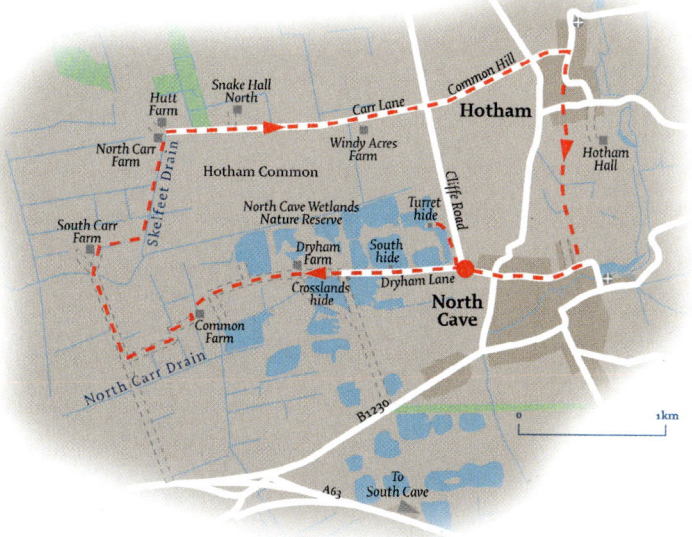

# Drewton Dale and St Austin's Stone

**Distance** 6km **Time** 2 hours
**Terrain** country roads, tracks and paths
**Map** OS Explorer 293 **Access** no public transport to the start

This walk through pleasant farmland on the edge of the Wolds takes you to a rocky outcrop which is said to be a site of pre-Christian worship, perhaps even giving the name of Druid's Town (Drewton) to the nearby settlement.

Start from Drewton Lane, the access road to Drewton Manor, off the A1034 Market Weighton road. Always keep the passing places clear and park with consideration on the grass verges. It is also possible to park at the Drewton Estate's nearby farm shop and walk on the wide verges of the A1034 to Drewton Lane but be aware of the shop and car park's opening times.

Head up the lane past the farm and Drewton Manor and bear left at the junction to pass a pond. Although it was mentioned in the Domesday Book, the settlement of Drewton was all but wiped out by the Black Death in the 14th century; the manor and estate farm date from the mid-19th century.

Continue uphill through the trees, looking out for red kites and buzzards, then follow the footpath sign right to go over a stile and across the field to a gap in the hedge. With good views across the

distant Humber opening up, carry on up along the edge of the woodland through Austin's Dale.

As you reach the end of the dale look out for the overgrown rocky outcrop of chalk and flint, about 20m into the woods, known as St Austin's Stone. As the rock is porous, water seeps out of it in places and in local folklore it is imbued with magical properties; part of it is said to fall away every seven years only for it to grow back.

According to local history, the rock was a sacred place for druids and is where St Augustine later preached and converted locals to Christianity, baptising them in a nearby well. Augustine was one of a group of monks sent from Rome who landed on the Kent coast in 597 on a mission to convert King Ethelbert and his kingdom. There's no record, however, of just how far north he travelled.

Follow the path out to the road, then briefly walk along the verge, looking out for traffic, before leaving it again on a signposted track. Skirt around a small woodland, then turn right to follow the footpath as it descends into a sunken lane, then crosses a field. Go around Diamond Cottage to return to Drewton Lane and follow it back to the start.

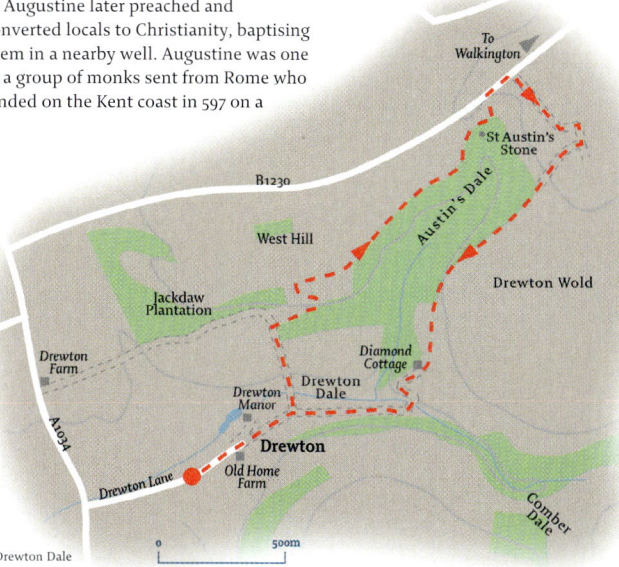

◀ Drewton Dale

# Hessle and Little Switzerland

**Distance** 3km **Time** 1 hour
**Terrain** pavement, tracks and paths
**Map** OS Explorer 293 **Access** Hessle railway station is 500m from the start

The Humber Bridge is the biggest single-span suspension bridge in the UK and the chalk cliff terraces of the nearby country park in Hessle are a great place to get a good view of it. This walk begins from the start point of the 127km-long **Wolds Way**, which ends in Filey in North Yorkshire, before touring the park and returning through residential streets.

Start the walk from the Wolds Way cairn by the car park (free) on the bend of Cliff Road in the shadow of the towering Humber Bridge. When the bridge linking Hull with North Lincolnshire was completed in 1981 it was the longest single-span suspension bridge in the world; today, the longest is the Canakkale Bridge in Turkey. Before the bridge a ferry crossing from here could take hours in bad weather.

Go under the bridge to reach Hessle Whiting Mill, built in 1810 to crush chalk from the nearby quarry and make it into whiting, at the time an ingredient in paint and putty. The mill is open to the public and there are displays inside on the history of the mill and quarry.

Follow the footpath by the mill under the road and into the oldest part of the country park, the site of the old chalk quarry. Known to locals as 'Little Switzerland', the park is a popular place with meadows, wildlife ponds and white chalk cliffs. The bright white cliffs which

surround the park on three sides gave the park its nickname; they were said to resemble the snow-covered Alps.

Follow the Chalk Way until you reach a sign for the Pond Trail, then go right to follow the Cliff and Pond Trail with the cliffs to the right. The nature reserve is home to 22 species of butterflies; the best places to see gatekeeper, meadow brown or comma butterflies are on the distinctive purple buddleia bushes. The ponds, which dry out in summer, are a good place to spot rare great crested newts which thrive as there are no predatory fish in the ponds. Please don't be tempted to capture or handle any newts you may see.

Go up the steps to the car park and follow the road towards the entrance, then take the gravel path under the bridge. Continue along a narrow residential street, then turn right at the end and continue towards the bend in Redcliff Road. Take the footpath just before the bend to return to Cliff Road and the start.

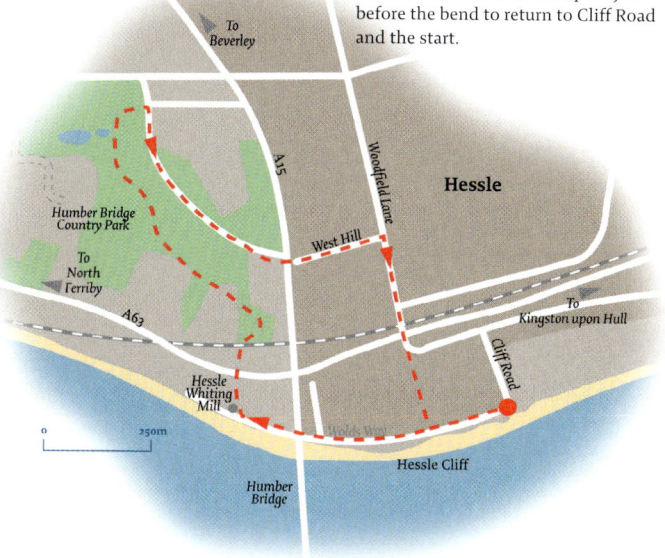

◀ Humber Bridge

# Kelsey Lakes

**Distance** 2.6km **Time** 1 hour
**Terrain** tracks and paths
**Map** OS Explorer 292 **Access** no public transport to the start

The flooded gravel pits of Kelsey Lakes to the east of Hull have been used for recreation since the 1960s and '70s; the larger southern lake was a popular place for water-skiing and is still known as the 'Ski Pond'. This walk skirts the ponds, then follows drainage ditches across low-lying farmland. Look out for swans, ducks, geese, herons, kingfishers, bitterns, owls and, if you are very lucky, osprey, as you make your way around this wildlife-rich wetland.

Start from the signposted car park at the end of the access road off Hariff Lane just south of Burstwick. Follow the track downhill past the fishing lake, then turn to follow the trail through a gate into the woodland to arrive at South Lake.

Formerly a popular spot with waterskiers, you are now more likely to see kayakers, canoeists, open-water swimmers and paddleboarders enjoying the still waters of 'Ski Pond'. These reclaimed gravel pits were principally dug in the 1850s to provide ballast for the building of the Hull to Withernsea railway line which carried Victorian workers and their families to the pleasure gardens and promenades of the seaside resort.

Continue along the side of the lake to the railway path with the houses of Keyingham in the distance, then follow the drainage channel through the former

marshland. Look out for deer, fox, rabbit and hares in the fields; the sound of the swaying reeds and bulrushes adds to the serene atmosphere.

This channel is part of a flood control system for the local area; the marshland was originally drained by four streams, or fleets, which have been widened, straightened and dredged to prevent future flooding.

The path along Keyingham Drain bends left to follow another drainage channel with the car park soon becoming visible; although it looks higher, it's only 15m above sea level. Continue past a concrete bridge, then turn left onto a track that goes gently uphill. When you are opposite the farm on the other side of the drain, look out for a path off to the left which leads back to the start.

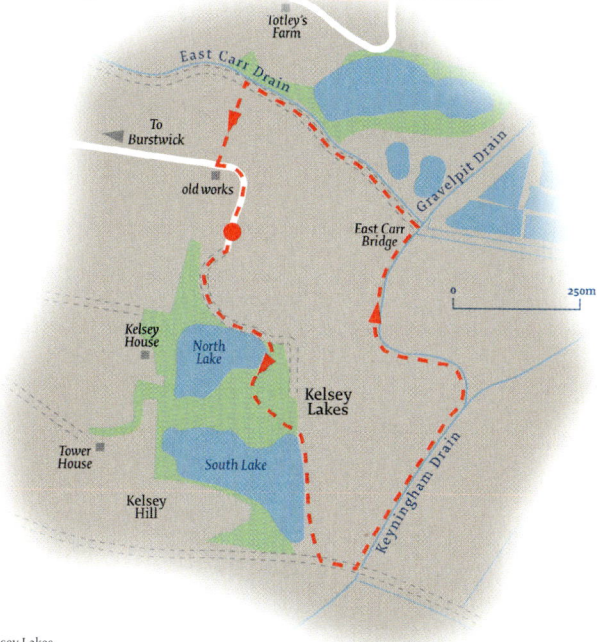

# Index

| | | | |
|---|---|---|---|
| Bainton | 44 | Malton | 58, 60 |
| Barmston | 24 | Market Weighton | 80 |
| Bempton Cliffs | 16 | Millington | 72 |
| Beverley | 84 | Nafferton | 46 |
| Bridlington | 22 | North Cave Wetlands | 88 |
| Buckton Cliffs | 16 | North Landing | 18 |
| Castle Howard | 62 | Norton-on-Derwent | 60 |
| Cherry Burton | 82 | Nunburnholme | 76 |
| Coneysthorpe | 62 | Octon | 34 |
| Cottam | 38 | Old Malton | 58 |
| Cowlam | 38 | Reighton | 14 |
| Dane's Dyke | 20 | Risby Park | 86 |
| Drewton Dale | 90 | Rudston | 40 |
| Driffield | 46 | Settrington Beacon | 56 |
| Flamborough | 18, 20 | Spurn Head | 28 |
| Flamborough Head | 18 | Sykes Monument, The | 42 |
| Filey | 10, 12 | Sylvan Dale | 72 |
| Fordon | 32 | Thirkleby Rattle | 36 |
| Foston on the Wolds | 48 | Thixendale | 68 |
| Goodmanham | 80 | Thwing | 34 |
| Gypsey Race, The | 36 | Wansford | 46 |
| Hessle | 92 | Warter | 76 |
| Hornsea Mere | 50 | West Lutton | 36 |
| Hotham | 88 | Westwood, The | 84 |
| Huggate | 70 | Wetwang | 42 |
| Hunmanby | 14 | Wharram-le-Street | 66 |
| Kelsey Lakes | 94 | Wharram Percy | 66 |
| Kilnsea | 28 | Wintringham | 54 |
| Kirkham Priory | 64 | Withernsea | 26 |
| Londesborough | 78 | Woldgate | 40 |